"No other book has provoked in me such spiritual wanderlust. From her unique perspective as an Afro-Caribbean woman, Quaker, Buddhist, and pilgrimage-lover, Valerie Brown celebrates the rich paradoxes of travel: exposure to the unfamiliar reminds us of the universal, and journeys into foreign terrain allow us to better know the landscape of home and self. Without ever packing a bag or leaving the comfort of my living room, what a wonderful pilgrimage to have traveled through the words, images, poetry, and faith of this book!"

— *Margaret Cooley, Executive Director, Woolman Hill, a Quaker retreat center*

"Each time that I returned to read more of *The Road*, I found my breath deepening and my soul opening, ever so gently. I love Valerie's wise opening, 'Every journey is both inward and outward.' Her writing invites both sensibilities. What a gift, as well, to have a black woman's perspective of this inner and outer journey within two spiritual traditions: Buddhism and Quakerism."

— *Niyonu D. Spann, founder, Beyond Diversity 101*

"It is a beautifully written book, imbued with honesty and insight by a fellow pilgrim—one who understands that spiritual preparation and reflection are an integral part of the path of pilgrimage—a practice of transformation. This book will inspire you to set off on journeys to places unknown to you to get to know who you are. Let it guide you."

— *Shantum Seth, Zen teacher and pilgrimage leader, Buddhapath Journeys*

"Valerie's unique and valuable voice draws on her Quakerism, her Afro-Caribbean heritage, her training in Buddhism, and her profound personal understanding of the transformative power of mindful travel. People who have an active, or budding, curiosity about pilgrimage will find helpful guidance from her on how to raise awareness and pay attention while away from home. Her teaching is strongly appreciated at Pendle Hill, and holding this book is akin to having her gentle teaching presence always nearby."

— *Jennifer Karsten, Executive Director, Pendle Hill, a Quaker retreat center*

"*The Road That Teaches* is an unusual travel book. Valerie Brown weaves the stories of her walking many of the great pilgrimages across the world with stories of a lifelong journey to more fully inhabit her own heart. Part detailed guide to great pilgrimages and part reflection on a lovingly examined life, this book explores her inner and outer experience in ways that both invite the reader along and inspire us to reflect on our own lives."

— *Terry Chadsey, Executive Director, Center for Courage & Renewal*

"Ghost Ranch in Abiquiu, New Mexico is a sacred place where early ancestral camps to modern human pilgrimages are framed in a geology that formed the inspiring landscape. Valerie Brown has a deep understanding of humanity's yearnings, a unique perspective on pilgrimage tra   and steward-ship of the land and its resources. She can both se   'transformation through travel.'"

— *Debra M. Hepler, e:*

"Valerie weaves mindfulness, Buddhism, and Quakerism together in telling the story of her meandering pilgrimages in Scotland, Japan, India, Spain, and New Zealand, taking the reader, as well, on inner journeys of the heart and spirit. Her observations of the natural world and her reflections on both the physical and spiritual path remind us to stay present to the moment—to meet what each step of the journey and each breath has to offer, right now."

— *Irene McHenry, PhD, executive director, Friends Council on Education*

"In the midst of people who feel a called to be seekers and pilgrims, some are called out from among us to be guides. Valerie Brown in her book *The Road That Teaches* becomes such a guide for the reader. Ms. Brown is a guide because she is a seeker, and a seeker because she believes in the call to daily spiritual practice. With transparency and honesty Ms. Brown interweaves her spiritual life lessons with threads of pilgrimage experiences from around the world. The threads form to create a wonderful book creating a beautiful tapestry of self awareness and serving as a guide for others who might risk true life pilgrimage. Ms. Brown has walked the road, risked to take the journey, and has thus becomes a guide for us as she opens in page after page the transformational gifts of travel."

— *Dr. Jean Richardson, director, Kirkridge Retreat and Study Center*

"Valerie Brown's unique African-Caribbean-Buddhist voice in this poetic and beautiful book brings a new perspective to the juxtaposition of pilgrimage with realization of the beauty and depth of the inner human landscape. Valerie is constantly teaching us the value of slowing down, of seeing deeply into an understanding of the beauty of who we are through her individual lens, through the ups and downs of parallel outer and inner journeying. She moves us through the joys and sorrows of pilgrimage and shows us how to use them for transformation."

— *Gina Sharpe, guiding teacher and co-founder,*
New York Insight Meditation Center

"The work of Valerie Brown dramatically shows the importance of pilgrimage in peacemaking. On pilgrimage the distant draws near and the stranger becomes a fellow pilgrim on life's sacred journey to a peaceful world. For this, Valerie Brown is a sure expert and guide."

— *Richard L. Deats, Emeritus Executive Secretary*
and Fellowship *editor of the Fellowship of Reconciliation*

The Road That Teaches

Lessons in Transformation through Travel

by
Valerie Brown

FGC

QUAKERBRIDGE PHILADELPHIA, PA

THE ROAD THAT TEACHES

Printed in the United States of America
QuakerBridge Media of Friends General Conference
1216 Arch Street, 2B
Philadelphia, PA 19107

Composition and design by David Botwinik

ISBN 978-1-937768-05-8

Library of Congress Cataloging-in-Publication Data
Brown, Valerie.
       The road that teaches : lessons in transformation through travel /
    by Valerie Brown.
           p. cm.
       ISBN 978-1-937768-05-8 (print)
       1. Travel—Religious aspects. 2. Pilgrims and pilgrimages. 3. Spiritual life.
4. Brown, Valerie--Travel. I. Title.
    BL628.8.B76 2012
    203'.51--dc23
                             2012028629

To order more copies of this publication or other Quaker titles call 1-800-966-4556
or visit the online catalog at **www.quakerbooks.org.**

For Trevor,
who was there for me at the right place and the right time.

Contents

AUTHOR'S PHOTOGRAPH RESOURCE
http://leadsmartcoaching.com/photo-gallery-2

ACKNOWLEDGEMENTS

I am a pen in the hands of God.
— Sufi proverb

Writing is sacred. It is an important bridge between the human and spiritual realms. It is an act of immense faith, hope, and love, laced with lopsided doses of deep gratitude.

This book would not be possible without the love, support, and encouragement of many people. I am grateful to my parents, Lewis and Trina Brown, from whom I inherited the spirit of wanderlust; to John Strachan, my husband, who typed, coached, and counseled me along the journey; to my family and especially my brothers Trevor, Lloyd, and Milton, who have always been a source of love, inspiration, and kindness; to my nieces and nephews Trevor Jemal Holltman, J. Holtham, Katie Lynne Brown, Kyle Brown, Amy Strachan, and Christopher Strachan. Thank you all for your love and support. My friends have been a huge source of encouragement and support, including Karen L. Erlichman and Kirsten Olson, as well as Sharon Victor and Abraham Leibson, my neighbors and friends, and Marisela Gomez and Brenda Harrington, kindred spirits. Thanks also to my friends Karen and Ben Marcune and Bill and Rene Taylor for their love and support over many years. My mentors have greatly shaped this book, including Parker J. Palmer and my long-time meditation and yoga teachers Mahan Rishi and Nibhe Kaur Singh Khalsa. My meditation and mindfulness practice has been greatly influenced by Thich Nhat Hanh.

Gratitude goes to my Dharma friends at Blue Cliff Monastery, Deer Park Monastery, Plum Village, and Old Path Sangha, and to the Quaker communities that have supported me, including Pendle Hill, Solebury Friends Meeting, and Woolman Hill.

For editorial assistance, I am grateful to Joan Broadfield, Barbara Mays, and Joan Lewis, who provided expert support and guidance. I am hugely grateful to the editorial staff at Friends General Conference, especially Chel Avery and David Botwinik.

I am indebted to the many retreat groups and many retreatants who have offered their love and listening ear.

Everyone needs a spiritual home and I am so lucky to have several, including Pendle Hill, the Center for Courage & Renewal, the Center for Transformational Leadership at Georgetown University, the Center for Mindfulness in Medicine, Health Care and Society, Kirkridge Retreat and Study Center; New York Insight Meditation Center, Ghost Ranch, Khalsa Healing Arts & Yoga Center, the Community of St. John Baptist, and St. Philip's Chapel.

I have received great comfort, rest and wonderment at the Chalfonte Hotel, Chanticleer and Bowman's Wildflower Preserve.

This book is dedicated to the living memory of my mother, Trina Brown; to Elaine Yuenger Brower and Beverly Fuller Garnett; and to my niece Brittany Marie Brown. Although they did not physically take these journeys, they taught me how to travel well.

INTRODUCTION

Journey Home

LESSON: Feeling "at home" in the world depends on one's state of mind.

Where we love is home.
Home that our feet may leave—
but not our hearts.

— Oliver Wendell Holmes

Every journey is both inward and outward, an opportunity to discover new meaning or encounter the world with fresh eyes. Pilgrimage, a special kind of travel, is a physical, geographical, and spiritual effort, akin to prayer. It is the individual and collective search for the sacred, where the spiritual experience and geography converge. A pilgrimage expresses a yearning of the heart to be in God's presence, the presence of the Holy. It points the self toward a destination—a sacred place. It is the physical embodiment of inclining the heart toward God.

Pilgrimage is not particularly Christian, European, African, Asian, or Medieval. It is a central feature of most world religions that goes back long before written records. It is a deep-seated human tendency to locate the Holy at a distance from one's everyday surroundings and to seek solutions to personal problems, alleviate suffering, keep a vow, mark a transition, or avoid boredom through a journey.

Pilgrimage is an encounter with life as it is. It is finding beauty and meaning in the very ordinary. Pilgrimage is about making meaning by journeying out and by journeying in with heart, mind, and soul.

The impulse to journey is part of the human spirit, blending a yearning with conviction toward the sacred. We may travel to obtain a physical objective, such as reaching a sacred shrine or destination. We may travel with hope and confidence that a new energy will be present, and bring long sought-after change. Perseverance and receptivity to new settings and to change are essential tools of the pilgrim's knapsack.

Whether pilgrimage is seen as a rite of passage or a defining moment, it is a time of crossing a threshold where, having unlatched a door, we enter a new and spiritually significant experience.

Pilgrimage journeys vary greatly. Buddhist pilgrims, for example, seek out sites associated with the life of Buddha. Every twelve years in India, Hindus travel to where the Rivers Ganges and Yamuna converge with the mythical underground Saraswati River for the Kumbh Mela—a cleansing pilgrimage— to Allahabad. The Golden Temple in Amritsar in India's Punjab is among the most sacred Sikh shrines. Many Jews journey to Jerusalem's Wailing Wall. Japanese pilgrims climb sacred mountains in homage to Shinto traditions.

Some say one begins the pilgrimage journey the moment one leaves the womb, journeying through time and space. Pilgrimage is a vestigial impulse that, like gravity, forever pulls us. This impulse is the experience of all humankind, which tends toward hope. Pilgrimage is a way of putting one's beliefs to the test, to grasp for meaning and purpose. It is a way to look at life itself with a willingness to alter fixed ideas about oneself, putting aside lifestyles, comfort, likes, and dislikes. Traveling on a steamy, crowded bus in a downpour in Delhi moved me from the idyllic fantasy of the Taj Mahal to the reality of solo travel.

I was raised by people who traveled. My Cuban mother, Jamaican father, and Chinese Trinidadian relatives gave me an early appreciation of the world as a large and complex place. Like many people who immigrated to America they were a liminal people, caught in a sort of limbo. Having left their native Caribbean land, they no longer belonged to their previous society and they were not fully incorporated into American culture. Like pilgrims, my parent's journey from their island countries to America was full of possibility, of social, psychological, and economic transformation, even if temporarily. Their arduous journey, with little more than a suitcase, was not unlike the pilgrim's journey. My parents came to America bearing the collective consciousness of their parents and their parents' parents, again not unlike the pilgrim who travels with a sense of *communitas*, a quality of togetherness, a shared encounter.

Perhaps most of all, my parents came to America with hope. It was hope that propelled them to leave their island lands. Hope was by their side as they made plans. Hope inspired their vision and colored their motivation. However, the other side of hope is fear, the fear of an unknown land, of not knowing people, customs, language, and food. This could have kept them immobilized and small. The writer Margaret Wheatley says, "Hope never enters the room without fear at its side." But like pilgrims, my parents endured the hardship, uncertainty, and insecurity. A pilgrim learns from doing, allowing the journey to be the goal. Fear and insecurity often provide energy, tools to figure things out along the way.

I discovered a pilgrim's heart and mind when I left home at eighteen after my mother's early and sudden death. Dazed and scared, I took very little with me—some clothes, a few dolls. I threw them in a sheet in the back of my boyfriend's pick-up and hit the road. The pain of leaving behind many meaningful possessions—the beautiful Vietnamese doll from my brother's tour of duty, my favorite sweater—stayed with me for many years. Overnight I left the safety and security of home and started my journey as a pilgrim to find the sacred center—a new home, my place in a complex world—without a guidebook, compass, or map.

I searched for a sense of home, a place of belonging in graduate school and law school, losing myself again and again in a well-ordered work life, on the straight and narrow path of an overambitious race to succeed in my career as an attorney. I rushed everywhere. My mantra was the words of actress Carrie Fisher: "Instant gratification takes too long." I craved control and predictability, trying to think my way out of the box I had created. Terrified by my childhood of poverty, I wanted to get going while the getting was good. I mistook a good job, a nice home, family, and friends for the home I left long ago. I forgot, or perhaps never learned, how to be in the world, how to listen to myself and others, how to love and feel fully alive. All the while, my sense of incompleteness persisted like a nagging cough.

A divorce years later forced me to look deeply at my ever-present incompleteness and unfulfilled longings. I studied meditation and yoga, enrolled in weekend courses on forgiveness, active listening, and authentic movement, returned to graduate school to study theology, found the writings of Thich Nhat Hanh, the Vietnamese Buddhist Zen Master, and became a Quaker. Slowly the fault line of fear and doubt that held me tight began to crack open, and I sensed a new possibility.

I would learn that leaving home was the formative ground for my interest in pilgrimage. Leaving home transported me out of the comfortable and familiar and into a wild card of fear, awe, terror, and wonder. I was as needy as a newborn but wouldn't admit it. In leaving home I learned the language of vulnerability, taking a leap of faith in some instances, testing my courage in others, and sinking into uncertainty and doubt.

On a visit to Stonehenge on the windswept and isolated Salisbury Plain, I was surprised, even disgusted, by the ropes cordoning off the stones from the tourists. After all the planning and dreaming, I stood facing the stones only to find them small and inaccessible. I thought about all those small, inaccessible places within me—the moments of fear and disappointment, the pride and shame. My frustration turned to quiet awareness, having touched a part of myself in the stones.

Leaving home was many things: a painful break with security, a time of self-discovery, an act of rebellion, a joyous adventure, a deep mystery, and a moment of wide open risk. Starting out on this journey was filled with hesitation and dark clouds of doubt, and yet I knew I was being called down an uncertain road.

Dark places and dark paths on my journey helped me to reclaim my life and unlearn old habits. Revelation came in gulps or sometimes with painfully slow insight. There were times on the road too when I laughed my head off. I hardly noticed what was happening. Step by step, I gained little glimpses into what I did not know or did not see was there all along. I was in a dynamic, living relationship with change and uncertainty on the footpath to transformation.

Sacred texts are filled with traveling stories, a metaphor for life. The excitement of leaving home and the call of the open road have long been considered coming of age tales of discovery, apprehension, and anticipation. My emotive heart said, "Come see."

Heracitus, the Greek philosopher, said we never step into the same river twice. Nothing stays the same. Everything changes, always. Traveling solo changed me. The first change was learning to slow down. When I really slow down enough to see and experience, I feel that I have fully arrived, and have a connection with the place and people. This slowing down can be physically moving slower as I walk, or it can be walking faster with greater awareness of each step, fully taking in the experience in mindfulness.

Leaving home is not for the faint-hearted. It may be scary and unpredictable. I leave home each time I see beyond the boundaries that mark the daily grind and dream something new into being. I leave home each time I look beyond old choices for clear-cut answers. The good news is that home is still there, waiting for me. Home is a state of mind. It is that light-filled place of love, trust, and faith that steadfastly guides me as I travel in the world.

Tourist Becomes Pilgrim

The mindful exert themselves;
They are not attached to any home;
Like swans they abandon the lake;
They leave home after home behind.

— Dhammapada

Long before the invention of the map or compass, pilgrims made their way by following lights—the stars and sun. The People of Israel wandered through the desert wilderness on their way to the Promised Land. Traveling tales speak of faith in the face of change, uncertainty, the unknown.

Pilgrim's faith on the road is akin to what Buddhists call the *beginner's mind*, the mind that notices and questions. It is the mind that looks into the unknown with openness—without a map or compass. As a traveling Quaker, I experience pilgrim journeys as an opportunity to live the power of a faith that recognizes God in every person, to witness the beauty and unique possibility of everyone I encounter.

Initially, my goal in traveling to faraway places was to pack it all in. I was cranky from pushing hard to get things done. I wanted to see the sights, to be entertained, to get away from it all. I traveled from one must see sight to another: the Taj Mahal, the Great Pyramids, Machu Picchu. Journeying from sub-Sahara Africa to Wales to Cuba became a search for entertainment, penny pinching every step of the way. Each sacred shrine, each place of devotion was just another curiosity stop. My passive metropolitan body sought a momentary recovery in these "power places," where I could get back to nature, connecting with my "inner-Indiana Jones."

After a much anticipated tour, arriving by bus and train at Cardiff Castle, in the Welsh capital, my schedule was so tight I barely had time to take in this ancient place. After all the planning, waiting and traveling, I saw very little and felt even less. The truth of the place was lost in the blur of hurry. The experience left me feeling like a run-down toy. In that moment I knew it was time to change.

My urge to take pilgrimages began with the need for rest, for more than a vacation, for real healing. I wanted to travel without a destination or agenda, to allow the luxury of time to unfold, to be lost in the small, ordinary moments and know that this is enough. I wanted to walk the pilgrim's path, to allow the uncertainty of the road—the bad weather, the getting lost—to strip me of the illusion of control and shatter my small self.

Gradually, traveling challenged me to look deeply at myself, at my gritty individuality, my practiced cynicism, at the status and resources I worked hard to acquire. Traveling allowed me to see beyond the cultural barriers (race, language, and custom) that divide me from others, and to look at the universal truth of all people, not only with a backpacker's spiritedness but with a wise heart.

People everywhere in the world, despite unique culture and custom, desire many of the same things: love, compassion, mercy, and kindness. We share a universal longing to be known, and being known, to be loved. Benedictine monk David Steindl-Rast in *The Great Circle Dance of the Religions* says, "The heart of every religion is the religion of the heart. . . . Heart stands here for the core of our being where we are one with ourselves, one with all, one even with the ground of our being." Pilgrimage travel has allowed me to really see the other, not only as separate from myself, but to recognize the bonds of mutuality.

I stood at the ruins at Machu Picchu in Peru and found God as the early morning fog lifted from the mountain to reveal the sacred lost city.

I found God in the girl trapped by a life of poverty selling Chicklets chewing gum on the streets of Quito, Ecuador.

I found God in the nomads of the White Desert in the Egyptian Sahara who carried their entire day's meal, their shelter, and prayer amulet in a drawstring camel sack around their necks.

I found God in the most holy temple of Boudhanath Stupa in Nepal, Kofukuji Temple in Japan, Borobudur Temple of Java, the Golden Temple in Amritsar, India, the Great Sphinx of Cairo, and the Anasazi cliff dwellings in Albuquerque, New Mexico.

I found God in the beautiful and complex dances of the native Balinese women.

In finding God in these places, I've passed beyond language to look deeply at myself and the other. I discovered the familiar in these foreign places and strengthened the spiritual foundation of my inner house, my spirit. Hardship and uncertainty of travel became the bricks and mortar; my intention and motivation became the roof.

Francis X. Clooney in *Praying Through the Non-Christian* raises questions I have asked myself:

○ How do I see *the other*?

○ Am I different when I return from a journey to *the other*'s faith?

○ How does embracing *the other* inform my faith?

Rather than stereotyping *the other*, it is important to "meet the other as myself." Meeting Muslims, Hindus, Sikhs, and Buddhists has expanded my consciousness and notions of home, seeing aspects of each religious tradition in myself. As a Quaker, I understood in a new and different way the belief that God resides in every person.

On a trip to Amritsar's Golden Temple, I was so focused on the formal etiquette associated with entering the *gurdwara* and chanting that I nearly missed the real connection with people. After a few days like this, I tucked away my dogged reliance on the rules and began to focus on the people. I fixed my eyes on an Indian woman in a flowing sari, feeling her beauty, dignity and calm. I learned that true religion is not naming oneself Buddhist, Christian, Hindu, Jew or any other; rather, it is our expression of love.

Denise Lardner Carmody and John Tully Carmody in *Prayer in World Religions* note:

> One may still feel the prostration or chant to be foreign, but the process of trying it on, struggling to make it one's own and expressing one's love or need through it, will greatly domesticate it. Just as those who visit a monastic chapel and spend a peaceful half hour learn something immensely important about monasticism, so those who sit in yoga or sacrifice a kola nut or experience the sweat lodge pass over a border and no longer feel like a complete outsider.

The God of my childhood has given way to the God of my womanhood, a God of many names: Allah, Shiva, Great Spirit, Lord Krishna, Lord Buddha, and Yahweh.

Pilgrimage is about quest for truth. There may be stories and anecdotes to exchange. There will be times too when the journey feels daunting, lonely or excitingly uncharted—like walking down an unfamiliar road in the darkest night. On a solo camping trip to Washington State's Mount Rainier, I pitched my tent near ancient hemlocks, massive and scarred by wind and snow. I felt insignificant, tiny next to them.

I began traveling as a seeker in search of knowledge and found the Holy in the most unlikely places—on a crowded train from Delhi to Jaipur, sleeping in the mud hut in a small village in Malawi, waiting in line to buy fresh bread at a local baker in

Assisi, and many more. I found what Celtic spirituality calls *thin places*: where heaven and earth touch, where God seems readily present, where the separation between the Holy and the ordinary is very thin. In all these places I discovered the paradox and the unexpected meaning of home. I found home in doing less and being more, in planning less of my day and discovering unexpected joy in allowing the day to unfold in its own rhythm. I found home sitting in the stillness of the early morning, in feeling the sun on my face in mid-day and looking up at the night sky with a wondering heart. Every journey is potentially spiritual, and—depending on my conscious awareness—is the path of love.

How to Use This Book

The Road That Teaches: Lessons in Transformation through Travel witnesses the power of the human spirit and the presence of God in ordinary and extraordinary moments through travel and especially pilgrimage journeys. It is written from my unique perspective as an Afro-Caribbean American, Quaker, and Buddhist woman. Each chapter is devoted to a different country (Spain, India, Scotland, Japan, New Zealand—places where I feel deeply connected to the land and to the people) and the last chapter is on nearby pilgrimages. Each chapter focuses on the wisdom of pilgrimage and lessons learned—not once but many times—on the road. Each chapter ends with lessons designed to inspire action in everyday life. The appendices include a traveler's packing list, sample training schedule for El Camino, and my top picks of travelers' resources.

Use this as a prayer book and guidebook for contemplation, discernment, and reflection. It may serve as a traveling companion and is meant to inspire and support spiritual journeys and travel of any kind, business or pleasure. It may be particularly useful for people who hate to travel, providing an opportunity to re-think the many gifts of travel. Ask questions, write reflections, and explore hidden longings in these pages. Use the Quaker-style queries (a series of questions and insights drawn from *Advices & Queries* which is used both for personal reflection and for reading aloud during meeting for worship) and Buddhist *gathas* (prayers or mindfulness verses recited throughout the day to restore mindfulness in daily life) to begin your internal discernment process and guide your reflection. Discover for yourself how travel can be transformative.

Author's Photograph Resource

See photos from my journeys at http://leadsmartcoaching.com/photo-gallery-2.

CHAPTER 1

Where the Wind Crosses the Stars

Pilgrimage of El Camino de Santiago

LESSON: Make haste slowly.

Travelers, there is no path; paths are made by walking.

— Antonio Machado

Every journey changes us in some way. It is hard to see this when we are in the midst of change. A glimpse of hope, a hint of a new way of seeing, amazement at a sudden change of heart may point to unexpected growth.

My pilgrimage on El Camino de Santiago, the Way of St. James, was an inner journey as much as an outer journey. While traveling had become as familiar as a TV jingle that kept playing in my head, the challenge of El Camino—walking sixty-two miles across the rugged north coast of Spain—placed me well outside my comfort zone to tolerate the ambiguity of the road and still hang in there in faith.

I learned about faith, loss and failure, security and hope, taking risks and making changes as I grew up. I was sixteen when my mother, my custodial parent, died suddenly. I grew up fast after that. I put aside high-school games to step into adulthood, but held onto my dreams of seeing the world. I made a deep promise to myself that one day I would discover the meaning of this loss.

El Camino tapped into the rhythmic clockwork of my heart. It challenged me to put aside the sharpened pencils in the pretty box on my desk and the books arranged in alphabetical order on the shelf in exchange for a touch of fear and the swift current of adventure.

Travel can be glorious and at times challenging. The latter all too often is most memorable. Once, on arriving at one of the many small hostels on the road while walking El Camino, I was attacked by a squadron of flies. It was so brutal that I placed a wet shirt around my head to outwit them and stay cool at the same time.

My journey to El Camino began with a deep desire and yearning. I had reached an emotional crossroad. My life felt like one big effort. Overachieving had taken a toll on my physical, emotional, and spiritual well-being.

Although I was traveling with three companions—Anna, Teresa, and Carla—I was scared; I worried that I would not be able to keep up and that I would get lost. I worried about not knowing enough Spanish and about where I would sleep. Would I have enough food, clothes, and equipment in my rucksack? I gave myself over to my inner voice that said, *Go*. I decided to travel with unanswered questions and a child's wide-eyed curiosity. El Camino was an opportunity to walk in the long daylight hours and the beauty of dusk, to be one of the followers of St. James who have walked this path for more than eleven centuries, to contemplate the path of my life that brought me to this place, and to be touched and transformed by little chapels and great cathedrals, by blue butterflies, and the Milky Way in the darkest night. At least this is what I told myself.

Ultimately, I learned to try underachieving—to live in the present moment, an important Buddhist teaching about mindfulness, a quality of nonjudgmental awareness of what is happening inside and outside. Mindfulness is not just a state of clear-headedness but also a quality of acceptance, openness, and ease. In mindfulness, I look squarely at what is now. Each step, if I am attentive, brings me to the present moment. Waking up, I am clearer, about possible direction, about choices.

They say miracles happen on El Camino, that this ancient path "does a person," not the other way around. Walking the endless track along a country lane with no farmhouses or farmer in sight, and not even the occasional pilgrim, I think surely this is the wrong road, or the way marker has been moved. As early morning turns into mid-day, the empty road gives way to one building and then another. My mood lightens. I'm reminded that on El Camino—like much of life's journey—my frustrations, doubts, and disappointments, large and small, are often my own making. How I see the world in front of me affects how I feel. I can approach each new landscape with life and transforming aliveness or with lead-footed deadness. It's about perspective.

History and Lore of El Camino

El Camino, the way to the holy city of Santiago de Compostela, lies in the northwest corner of Spain. The city's magnificent Romanesque cathedral contains the remains of St. James, the first cousin of Jesus Christ and one of the twelve apostles. James was beheaded in 44 A.D. in Jerusalem. The stories and legends of El Camino have created a rich body of folklore. Ninth-century religious hermit Pelayo, who was searching for the source of a strange, starry light over what is present-day Compostela, discovered the apostle's long forgotten tomb in a dense forest. How did the body of St. James get there from Jerusalem? The answer is one of the most remarkable stories of medieval times.

After James was beheaded, two of his disciples gathered up his remains and placed them in a stone boat. They set sail for Hispania, where James was said to have proselytized during his lifetime, and arrived on Galicia's Costa de Morte before sailing upstream to the present day Padrón. His body was then moved inland some twenty kilometers, buried on Mount Libredon, and then forgotten until Pelayo's faithful discovery eight centuries later. The tale of St. James has been embellished over the centuries, and faith drove millions of pilgrims to undertake the long, arduous journey to Santiago.[1]

A half million pilgrims journeyed each year at the height of Santiago's popularity in the eleventh and twelfth centuries.[2] It is even said that the road to Europe was formed by El Camino. They made the journey for devotion: to acquire merit, as a form of afterlife insurance against eternal damnation, to keep a solemn vow, to seek healing for themselves or others, to express gratitude, as penance, in hope of redemption, in bereavement, or in liberation at the end of a personal crisis.

It is said that El Camino is measured not in miles but in the spirit in which you walk. Discovering the truth of this statement was one of many life lessons on El Camino. Day after day we walked along, arriving just before nightfall to the *refugios*, pilgrim hostels. I was dirty, my clothes were grungy, and my boots were caked with mud. I was tired of wrapping my feet with Vaseline, moleskin, and lamb's wool. I was sick of arriving at the *refugios* only to find the only bed available is the top of five stacked to the ceiling, the mattress ripped and filthy. I stand waiting in line to use the shower which is caked with grime and smelly, the walls splattered with dead flies. I sleep with one eye open clutching my rucksack for fear of having my

---

[1] Edwin Mullins, *The Pilgrimage to Santiago* (New York: Taplinger Publishing Company, 1974), pp. 8–11.

[2] Antonio Vinayo Gonzalez, *The Pilgrim Route to Santiago, A Practical Guide* (León, Spain: Ediciones Leonesas SA "Edilesa," 1999), pp. 76–77.

passport stolen, not letting my boots out of my sight. I'm beginning to feel like a homeless person, like the poverty-stricken girl of my childhood. Packing and unpacking my sparse belongings and eating day-old food buried in the bottom of my rucksack left me feeling destitute. I could walk away from all of this, pull out my American Express card and find the nearest Sheraton. Cut and run has been my strategy in life, what I'm most comfortable doing. Here, on El Camino, I face this impulse, and bless it.

The next morning I walked outside the *refugios* to be greeted by the sun.

Of the three pilgrimages in the Middle Ages—Jerusalem, Rome, and Santiago de Compostela—the latter is the longest, most traveled, and most evocative pilgrim route in Europe. There are two popular routes. The left route, with its romantically beautiful landscape, ascends the Cizur Pass and is said to have been used in the Middle Ages. The right route begins at the Right Bank in Paris and the village of Pied-de-Port, crossing the Pyrenees and entering Spain at Roncesvalles. The route to Santiago is an ancient Roman trade route. It was nicknamed *la Via Lactéae*, the Milky Way—and the road under the stars which led the way to the edge of the known world, where the sun descended. The medieval pilgrim attached importance to the relics of saints, martyrs, and apostles. They sought to go to the ends of the earth to insure a place in the kingdom of God. Unlike a Muslim pilgrimage or *hajj* where the emphasis is on intention, in this pilgrimage the emphasis is on completion despite adversity, reaching the city of Santiago and obtaining the Compostela, an official recognition from the church that one has completed the pilgrimage.

Early pilgrims wanted not just to be in the physical presence of holy places, objects, and persons, but to absorb this spiritual power—to touch the sacred with hands and feet, to kiss the sanctified earth, to see, hear, touch, and feel, to connect with the *loca sancta* (the holy place) not just as a mark of the Divine or to gain a blessing but to be transformed. I knew the deep transformation I craved could not be achieved as a casual tourist looking for a "travel-poster picture and experience." Traveling no longer meant racking up miles, or a sense of adventure, or a desire to see the world. Instead, by traveling I became a spiritual "activist," committed to finding what was genuinely true and meaningful, to getting to know the half-seen, half-understood parts of myself through the eyes of others.

From a Quaker perspective, I focus on the queries, the questions that motivate my travel: *Why do I want to travel to this place now? Does travel satisfy a strong desire? What are my emotions? Am I being called on the pilgrimage? Is this a calling into faithfulness?*

El Camino, the Way, invited me to ask many questions: *Which way do I go? What am I seeing? What do I give my energy to?* These are geographical, moral, and spiritual questions. For many, and for me, the reasons for this journey were unclear, even unnamable, and could change from day-to-day, moment-to-moment. To walk the pilgrim path is to throw my arms around mystery, to offer each day as an opportunity to unfold into being. Maps, cairns, and routes point the way. The "way" rises out of seeing and being in the world.

Buddhists often refer to "bare noting"—noticing without reacting or responding to what is present, being grounded in the sense of pure awareness and attentiveness. This awareness—noting the green grass, tasting cool water, feeling my heavy pack—is a spiritual practice. Breathing and resting in what is already here is enough. This Buddhist practice has a way of opening the heart and relaxing the mind. Bare noting allows me to see clearly without immediately rushing to do something. I can choose to respond, to take action from the stillness of an open heart and mind—or not. On El Camino something happens in the simplicity and the immediacy of just walking day-after-day. All my belongings are in a rucksack on my back. The beauty behind is gone. I keep my attention on what is in front of me now. Effort and passion meet on the road and within me. One learns to be grateful and to love what comes your way, and take it easy.

I'm passionate about food. Back home, I'm called a purist because I make yogurt, fresh-baked bread, and granola from scratch, grow vegetables from seeds, and dry peppers. On El Camino I worry about getting good, healthy food. Some pilgrims cook meals with food they carry. Often we eat at local bars serving fried pork or beef and white bread with cheese. It's filling and cheap. After a few days like that we opt for dinner at a nice restaurant but find, after walking eight miles into town, that it closed at four o'clock. Walking another half mile, we arrive at a family-run establishment that just opened. I stuff myself on garlic soup, fish stew and chocolate covered fruit. On El Camino, I live the mixed bag of acceptance and gratitude, to love what comes my way, finding tenderness in unexpected places.

Preparation for the Pilgrimage: Walking Rules

We thirst at first.

— Emily Dickinson

I came to this pilgrimage by a chance meeting with a Cuban woman who responded to an ad I posted in my local health club to split my share in an organic farm. When Carla visited my home, she saw my numerous books on El Camino. As it turned out, she was planning to do the walk with two of her high school friends, Anna and Teresa, from Cuba, now living in Texas and Georgia. We cinched the idea of traveling together when I revealed my Cuban background. I asked if I could join the group, and we began to plan our trip together.

I love the rhythm of walking, the spirit of freedom, and the discipline that comes with a good day's walk. I love the cleansing and therapeutic follow-the-line-on-the-horizon-past-fields-and-barns feeling. I love the feel of my boots on dusty roads, the way my rucksack shifts slightly from one side to another as I move my hips. I love the feeling of having "shut the door" at least for the moment on work and responsibilities. I love the simplicity of focusing on one step and then another. I love the momentary brushes with kindness and unexpected happiness. I love the feeling of trust that if I give away my last plum, five miles down the road a plum tree will appear. I can lose a sense of weighty responsibility to the call of the road. Every hill, every bend in the road is a new invitation.

Preparation for El Camino is almost as important as the journey. I needed to prepare my emotional heart even before I bought my plane ticket. I committed to three essential daily practices that I would continue on the path: daily journaling, reflection, and inviting transformation. In journaling about small insights and daily awareness, unearthing the mess of emotions felt raw as I stared down the neglected parts of myself, the wanting to heal and not knowing how, the unexplainable wave of discontent and pain that kept surfacing. Reflection on a range of emotions—from disappointment to boredom, from haughtiness to helplessness—when combined with acceptance opened the door, even a tiny crack, to new insights. In this process of observing, writing, and reflecting, I learned how to listen and, fumbling at first, to train my heart to be attentive. In inviting transformation, I would allow all I had seen and done to work its alchemical magic on me.

Physical preparation for El Camino is critical too. I trained from April to mid-September, walking everywhere with a twenty-pound rucksack, cycling, and practicing Kundalini yoga and meditation. As a Kundalini yoga teacher, I relied heavily on both yoga and meditation as my foundation for training.[3] Traveling—sitting on flights, carrying bags across my shoulders, standing on bus or train lines—can wreak havoc on my body. Moving from place to place can leave me feeling spacey, anxious, and unsettled. To regain a sense of grounded-ness in my daily Kundalini yoga practice, I would visualize myself feeling rooted, hugging the muscles toward the bone, and focusing on deepening my breath. The week before my departure, I loaded my pack to do a test run at a nearby mountain range. I floated up the mountain without effort. I was strong, flexible, and confident in my physical abilities. Like many, I came to the pilgrimage believing that the challenge of walking for many miles over many days would make me stronger, healthier, and more balanced. I was in my early forties, not exactly young. I was to learn, instead, that El Camino was not so much about physical strength as it was about paying attention and trusting my heart.

While I was confident in these abilities, I agonized over what to take and what to leave behind.[4] I weighed toothpaste and socks. I searched for the right clothing and equipment. I resisted the temptation to spend hundreds of dollars on the latest high-tech, fashionable, ultra-lightweight clothing, and relied instead on accessories with a proven track record over time. I took no GPS units, no morning-after pills, no throw-away cameras, no laptop computer, no iPod, no games or musical instruments, and no books. The pack-rat instinct doesn't work on El Camino. I did take foot comforts: mole foam, moleskin, padded socks, lamb's wool to stuff between my toes, and bandages to wrap places where my boot might rub against my ankle or heel.

Some pilgrims say there are a few rules of the road. These I took seriously:

○ Carry less than you think you will need.

[3] See El Camino Training Schedule at Appendix I.
[4] See El Camino Packing List at Appendix II.

- ❍ Cut this by half.
- ❍ Reduce that amount by one-third.

The weight of my rucksack was an all-important decision. I opted to forgo carrying a tent, sleeping bag, and a sleeping mat, which would have weighed over ten pounds alone. I instead trusted the bare minimum:

- ❍ Two pairs of pants, one short and one long
- ❍ One short-sleeved shirt
- ❍ One long-sleeved shirt
- ❍ One fleece sweater vest
- ❍ Two pairs of socks
- ❍ One pair of sock liners
- ❍ One set of wicking undergarments
- ❍ Three pens and one notebook
- ❍ One cup
- ❍ One contact lens case
- ❍ One container of contact lens solution
- ❍ One quick-dry cloth
- ❍ One toothbrush and tube of toothpaste
- ❍ One bandana
- ❍ One pair of boots
- ❍ One pair of sandals
- ❍ Two panties
- ❍ Two bras
- ❍ One lipstick
- ❍ One pressed powder make-up
- ❍ One stick of deodorant
- ❍ One camera
- ❍ One brush

- One wallet containing passport, money, credit card, and pilgrim's credentials
- One watch
- One pair of earrings
- One turquoise necklace (my favorite stone)

My pack weighed in at twenty-six pounds.

Pilgrims call the knowledge of what to keep and what to leave behind "walking rules." Knowing what to take for the journey creates internal lightness and a quality of freedom that helps me to notice what takes me away from what matters most. Walking rules offer useful lessons in life, not just on the road. Knowing when and what to let go of is an essential element of freedom, focus, and growth. On the road as in life, it is important to know what is no longer useful, what is just taking up space, and what might be good and helpful but not the best use of my time. I know intuitively that sometimes I have to face losing something to get the freedom to do the right thing. It helps me get my "spiritual house" in order to ask: *Am I a religious consumer looking for a spiritual experience? As a pilgrim, am I living in God's presence daily? What habits do I need to put aside to put my trust in God? Where is the Inner Light in this pilgrimage, in the planning and packing?* In all the packing and deciding, I discovered an important truth: no matter what I take or leave behind, I will arrive at El Camino a pilgrim.

They say that miracles happen to the *peregrino* or pilgrim along El Camino and that *peregrinos* are protected along the path by their holy endeavor. My first miracle happened even before I left my home. After completing an exercise class at the local health club, I went to the front desk to collect my pass. The attendant handed me a book on the El Camino. Apparently, a man in the adjoining town read an article about my impending journey and decided to leave the book for me. I was already on the path.

Starting on the Journey

God carried you, just as one carries a child, all the way that you traveled until you reached this place.

— Deut. 1:31

We began the journey to Santiago in Madrid, taking the train to Pamplona, the city made famous by the running of the bulls, because we had allotted a mere two weeks for the trip. We would have only a taste of El Camino. I left behind my work life to enter a parallel universe, feeling the weight of my rucksack and my boots on the ground, confirming what is real. The walk from Pamplona to Cizur Major took us through parks and the university, slowly leaving behind the city and entering the valley.

The first step in taking a journey begins with starting. John O'Donohue in his book *To Bless the Space Between Us* tells the story of this beginning point. The setting is Connamara, Ireland. One neighbor had just begun to build his new home. He had stripped the sod off the field to begin digging out the foundation when an old man from the village happened to walk by. He blessed the work and said, "You have the worst of it behind you." The builder laughed and said, "I have only just begun." The old man leaned forward and said, "That's what I mean: you have begun and to make a real beginning is the most difficult act."

Before you begin there is a gestation period where you mull things over. There is hesitation, procrastination. You can talk yourself out of beginning. The German poet Goethe said that once a person commits, destiny conspires with us to support and realize our commitment. There is something impressive about a new beginning—a fresh start, a second wind, the beginning of a journey. Even before you have arrived for the start of the journey, there is the knowing that you have committed yourself.

In preparing for a journey, I am always reminded of the words of that wise and ancient sage, Woody Allen, who said, "Eighty percent of success is just showing up." This is the first rule of enlightenment.

The Spanish, of course, are famous for their long afternoon siestas; the entire country closes down from 1 to 5 p.m. and then reopens for business until 7 or 9 p.m. Arriving our first day at Pamplona, my traveling companions had a craving for *tocino del cielo*, a dessert they remembered from their childhood. It is nicknamed "bacon from heaven" because the light pastry is made of eggs and syrup. Carla found it in a nearby bakery, and we made our first plans to return to the bakery right after we obtained our pilgrimage credentials to certify our intention to perform a pilgrimage. These credentials are stamped at each *albergue*, or hostel, keeping a record of the pilgrim's journey. When we returned to the bakery after 2 p.m., it was closed. The lesson of the day: disappointment is a part of life.

Cravings, whether for *tocino del cielo* or for peace of mind, can be binding—a set-up for disappointment. Clinging out of fear or attachment to sense pleasures—delicious food, pleasant body sensations, my opinions and beliefs, or even spiritual practices—have kept me frustrated, wanting experiences to be different from what they are. I've been long-conditioned to shun my anger, to judge it as bad and nonspiritual, to believe that sadness is a problem to be fixed. I'm conditioned to believe that there is a shortcut to a spiritual life, like fast-food or instant coffee. The reality is that there no quick and dirty spirituality. The process of growing into a spiritual life is, like baking bread or blowing glass or throwing a pot on a potter's wheel, a creative unfolding that becomes strengthened by venturing down into the dark crevices of emotions: about the childhood we wanted but didn't have; the job that squeezes us dry; the relationships we want and the relationships we actually have.

Growth germinates in the seedbed of turmoil, calling us to embrace it, understand it, learn from it.

Buddhists recognize suffering as part of a full range of human emotions. In the face of anger, frustration, and disappointment, I have learned the hard way to cultivate acceptance. Resistance can be refusal to give up one thing for the sake of another—an unwillingness to change to allow myself to move into uncharted waters, or to sacrifice something I want to do. Acceptance is the price of every choice in life. On El Camino, I learned gradually to accept my anger, resistance, and frustrations. As a Quaker, I seek to bring my values and actions under the healing Inward Light, knowing that the present time is the right and best time to live in love, to learn from others along the pilgrim path, and to seek in all things the Inward Light as the source of my actions (not always, but often).

Many life situations draw pilgrims to walk El Camino. Some see it as a way to reflect before or after a divorce, to set off on a new journey when the kids are grown and gone, or after a long-time relationship or job has ended. There is an institutional order along El Camino with its well-organized *albergues* and well-ordered rules. And yet, there is a high-energy spirit of camaraderie and *communitas*, a chaotic and charitable energy, an interesting blend of competitiveness and conviviality. The locals, some worn weary by the parade of sunburned travelers, roast peppers on steel drums along the roadside. The locals labor over well-tended vegetable gardens or sit in groups of three and four in the village square until the sun casts deep lavender shadows. Brazilians, Spaniards, French, Germans, and New Zealanders walked along—an assemblage of drying underwear and flip flops dangling like ripe fruit from their packs.

In ancient times and today, pilgrims wear the shell of the sea scallop, sometimes as a "cockleshell" hat or sewn on a cape, as a way of acknowledging fellow pilgrims. The scallop is associated in legend with a miracle of St. James and is a symbol of a sacred passage to a venerable antiquity, an arduous and often life-threatening journey. In tradition, the scallop shell was also useful for pilgrims on El Camino de Santiago. It was the right size for gathering drinking water or for receiving scraps of food from the people along the way: a size so small that even the poorest could afford to give out of charity. Today, some pilgrims look stone-faced, some wear crystal and incense, and some adorn themselves with tattoos or diamond-studded nose rings.

At each encounter along the way conversation usually turned to feet, knees, backs, and especially blisters. My feet had long been toughened and calloused (one time calluses are a good thing), but just to be careful I wrapped each toe with moleskin, stuffed the space between them with lamb's wool, and covered the larger surfaces of metatarsal and heel with mole foam as protection for the journey. Pilgrims also talked about the road, and who took the wrong turn coming into town.

In earlier times pilgrims also anticipated hardship along the path, kneeling or fasting to arrive at holy ground with a pure heart and mind. To secure safe passage, these pilgrims often obtained written authorization from their bishop to make a pilgrimage. The spirit of these early pilgrims stayed with me in the form of questions: *What do hardship, frustration, unrealized dreams, teach me? Who has blessed my pilgrimage and who have I blessed today? How do I arrive at holy ground? Is the linkage between spiritual growth and suffering overrated?*

Like uneaten bits of food in the corner of the plate, the pilgrim feels unfinished until her official credential is stamped by the *albergue* host. Each step, each memory is memorialized in the credential, and without it one cannot receive the Compostela, obtaining official recognition from the church for having made the pilgrimage. One must walk a minimum of the last one hundred kilometers or cycle five hundred kilometers of El Camino to receive the Compostela. Pilgrims walk El Camino straight through, taking four to six weeks. Others cycle or ride horseback. Some make it an annual trip.

Along El Camino is a place where autumn crocuses gaze up from sandy footpaths, where lavender, thyme, and rosemary brush against my leg. It is a place to pick figs and grapes, to feel heavy boots, to savor cold water from village fountains and from gargoyles springing forth water at the bishop's house. Here I lie prostrate on the ground soaking in the scents, savoring peach and pear trees, olive trees and oleander, and the blossoms of sweet orange. It is a place to crush wild thyme under my heel.

Alto del Perdón (the Place Where the Wind Crosses the Stars) delights with its sleeping villages with names like Zariquiegui, Uterga, and Muruźabel. Windmills placed like matchsticks stretch out onto the horizon, coming as a surprise as we approached a steep ridge—a reminder of the unexpected. This is a beautiful place. I've come to appreciate these small places, each with their main plaza, narrow streets, and church tower.

For many years, I lived in a 900-square-foot historic house in central New Jersey. The house, built in 1873, was said to have been a candy store for the urban, now gentrified neighborhood, and was lovingly restored by the prior owners. The beauty of this small place was apparent the moment you walked through the front door: tin ceilings, stained-glass windows, a cast iron wood stove in the living room, and the kitchen painted in shades of sage green with black and white tiled floor. My friend Beverly painted fiddleheads and ostrich fern on one wall in the kitchen—homage to her garden. Living there all those years, I learned to appreciate and savor smallness, to be grateful for not having a lawn, for not having space for a wide-screen TV and entertainment center. The smallness of the place left me with time and energy to create something beautiful. I learned about wholeheartedness: living with one's whole heart and mind, living so fully that everyday, commonplace events become prayerful, treasuring what is in plain sight and being grateful. I could easily have focused on what I didn't have, and actually I did for too many years. Then I woke up. I can't remember the exact moment. I do recall one day being in the kitchen, listening to an old Richie Havens CD and thinking: "I'm so lucky."

We spent the night in the quiet village of Obanos. This was the opening night of the *albergue*, a medieval castle with hand-finished *viga* beams and Spanish-tiled floors, now converted into housing for *peregrinos*. Dining on anchovies, tomatoes, French bread, chocolates with hazelnuts, and aged cheese from the local grocery, we fell asleep in homey togetherness to the sound of church bells.

Obanos to Puente la Reina and Estella

The Puente la Reina (Queen's Bridge) took us toward a greener and richer texture as we left Navarra and entered La Rioja, Spain's rich wine-growing region. Row upon row of heavy, blue grapes stretched out in front of us. We crossed Puente la Reina's six-span Romanesque bridge as the Way of St. James continued past plowed fields—with basketball-sized garden cabbages, and olive and fig orchards—to Cirauqui. We trod on stones of the old Roman road and past snails crawling on dill weed on our way to Estella (Stellar), an ancient town well stocked with good cheese, bread, and the best wine of La Rioja. Its streets were crowded with convents and squares, a good place to spend the night.

Estella to Los Arcos and Logroño

You desire to know the art of living, my friend?
It is contained in one phrase: Make use of suffering.

— Henri-Frédéric Amiel

Leaving Estella, the third day, I walked until the weight of my pack began to rest heavily on my shoulders. We came to a fountain of wine and fresh spring water at Bodegas Irache, another miracle on El Camino. Irache is a twelfth-century Benedictine monastery dedicated to Our Lady of the Royal that is said to be the oldest in this region. Continuing through vineyards, we arrived at Villamayor de Monjardín for lunch in the ruins of the twelfth-century Romanesque St. Andrews Church.

Our first taste of a Spanish thunderstorm came as we walked the wide plains to Los Arcos. Standing in a downpour, our boots were caked with red clay soil, and the path was now a small river. Our pace slowed from a walk to a crawl. I was totally soaked, water filled the cracks in my boots and droplets plopped off the tip of my nose into puddles around me. I mumbled something under my breath about being in the present moment.

In Zen circles, archery is the study of precision and accuracy. The key is not to try to hit the target, but instead to draw the bow to the point of tension and allow the shot to release itself. My tendency when faced with the hardship of the road or work is to solve the problem quickly to avoid feeling the tension of not knowing what to do or say. Zen teachers say that spiritual growth, a new direction, arises out of these moments of tension. Allowing ourselves to feel the tension, the uncertainty, produces a kind of "inner ferment," often feeling raw, tender, and vulnerable. The arrow slips from our hand. Something new is born.

We entered Los Arcos only to find that every room in the town was filled, and we had no choice but to take a bus to the next town, Logroño, where we arrived for the Feast of San Martin. Here, too, we found every room in the town filled. In desperation, we decided to go to the *albergue*, taking a white Mercedes taxi to its front door and hoping that they would take us in for the night. The innkeeper was decidedly skeptical. He was abrupt and suspicious, but by the end of the evening we were sharing a bowl of powdered vegetable soup and trading stories. Another miracle along El Camino and an important lesson: the more you offer yourself to the world, the more the world offers itself to you.

Logroño to Ventosa: Make Haste Slowly

One must be able to let things happen.

— C.G. Jung

The art of pilgrimage is the art of slowing down, not speeding up. When I slow down, I move from chronological time into *kairos* time, from setting goals to soaking up experience, from doing to being. I touch the ultimate dimension, the sacred in the everyday. But slowing down does not come naturally to me. I grew up in New York City. I eat fast, walk fast. People say I talk fast at times. All this rushing made my initial efforts at meditation torturous. No sooner had I sat down on my *zafu* when my mind would wander to a torrent of thoughts: *What was that sound? Will I have enough milk for breakfast? My knee hurts. I want gum.* And so on. The thoughts came persistently, uncontrollably. Over time, I trained myself to say, *yes—I see this thought.* And then I would just put it down—like closing a book—coming back to the sensation of the breath and the feeling of my arms and legs. The rush of thoughts that mirrored my rushed life grew dimmer over time and less demanding—still there, but quieter.

At the *albergue* we are asked to leave promptly at 8 a.m. Most *peregrinos* eagerly set out on their way, tiptoeing about before dawn knowing the road ahead is long. My companions, however, didn't seem to be able to do anything before a "simple" breakfast of *café con leche*, tortilla, French pastries, and freshly squeezed orange juice. Rolling my eyes, I ate little or nothing. I was anxious and irritated, sick of the small talk. I wanted to get on the road, turn on my heels and get out of there. After all, we were here to walk. I could see it happening: around 2 p.m. they would say they are exhausted after walking eight miles, and must find the nearest *albergue*. My frustration piled up like the miles ahead of us. It was now the third or fourth day in this pattern: out at 8 or 8:30 a.m., breakfast until 9:30 or 10 a.m., stop to talk to anything that breathes, lunch at noon, stop again at 2 p.m. for more food, panic sets in, walk another couple miles, call the nearest hotel in exhaustion. My old habits were stronger than my will. I seriously contemplated ditching the others and striking out alone, at my pace. It's easier for me to walk away. It took patience and understanding to be accepting, and my skills here were rusty. The old pattern in me reemerged: push hard to "get things done."

What is the right pace, the right speed? If I go too fast, I risk injury. If I go too slowly, we might arrive too late to get a bunk in the *albergues*. Often, I ended up scrambling for a place to sleep, hastily taking care to bandage my feet, wash clothes, and talk about the weather with fellow pilgrims. Then suddenly I stopped dead in my tracks in the middle of the road. I asked, *Why am I in a hurry? Why do I need to leave at 5 a.m. in pitch darkness when everyone else waits for the first light to appear?* My inner emphasis on speed is about fear: the fear of missing out, the fear of not having my needs met, the belief that moving faster will lead to a better experience. I'll see more, do more, and be happier.

Much of my frustration is fueled by my sense of time, or lack of it. Even here I have a nagging sense of time slipping away. I admit I have a strange relationship with time. Despite all the rushing, I am perpetually late. I live with self-imposed deadlines to move faster, see more, and do more. Even though I am temporarily free of phone calls, emails to return, and meetings to attend, I feel the need to hurry up, press forward, move faster, look for the quick fix, and jump into the mad dash so as not to be left behind. Following this thread back to its roots, I realize that this internal pressure, like a car stuck in drive, comes from a deep encounter with the brute fact that I got a bum deal as a kid, that justice and fairness are beside the point, and that no one is going to make it up to me. I know too that I am who I am because someone loved me, and I bring into my life what I am most clear about. In walking this path, I get clear about what I want, what's important and why, and what's missing. I silently say a prayer of gratitude to those who have loved me.

Pilgrims in medieval times faced danger on the road: attacks by thieves, sickness. Life back home is filled with predictable routines: shower, breakfast in the car or at the office, return home, exercise, make dinner, sleep, and do this all over again. On El Camino each day brings unplanned, unexpected detours. I live in the freedom of the world without a minute hand, an extraordinary relationship to time for me.

Time unfolds. On the road, I am training in "be here now." Starting out after a brief rest, my attention lingers on the beauty of wild chestnuts drying on the hay in the afternoon sun. I slow my pace enough to allow my "soul to catch up to my feet." I'm staying with it all—the nice, the not so nice, the headache, and being happy. I accept yet another lesson on El Camino: spaciousness of heart and mind, being in God's presence, requires slowing down. Borrowing from the words of Thomas Merton, soul work requires "time to browse around." Pilgrimage is not about *where* one takes a journey, but *how* one travels. It is not so much about what we *do* as what we *are*. In slowing down, I hardly noticed the change as it happened. I got little glimpses of what I did not go to see or know was there. Slowing down allowed for interruption and surprise in unlikely places. It was like falling in love with the whole world. "Everywhere is in walking distance, if you have the time," says

Stephen Wright, the comedian. My lesson this day was about the gift of time in slowing down. My been-there-done-that mind gave way to vital awareness that everything I do this day is in God's presence. Awareness of the Inward Light is not awareness of a pious little niche in my day and pious little thoughts, but of an illuminated encounter with Spirit that springs from attentiveness. This conviction challenges me to examine my ingrained habits and attitudes. The first aspect of slowing down has been to notice my beliefs, and the second to admit that all my rushing was doing great harm to me. In learning to slow down, I learned an important lesson about the Quaker testimony on peace. Nonviolence begins with me, with accepting myself and others.

Somewhere along the way, I gave up the resistance to the struggle and decided to stop swimming against the current and accept my companions' pace and rhythm. In letting go, I put aside my goals and structure to be open to what El Camino has to teach me. Like a door opening, I realized that the path is the goal. Be prepared and then let go of expectations, El Camino taught.

In the process I learned that the pilgrim's path is pock-marked with unpredictability. I had planned and trained for hardship. I had read about El Camino and envisioned a clear-cut path ahead. What I had not planned for was unforeseen happiness. Instead of seeing my companions' pace as "wasting time" and trying to speed through the parts of the day that I saw as insignificant, I discovered an important insight about myself. El Camino revealed in raw detail my anxieties and my impatient, critical, and judgmental mind. Buried beneath all this was the fear that my fragile dream of finding true meaning from this journey would go unrealized. I believed that if I did not move as quickly as I could I would miss out on some unknown treasure. Far from missing out, I learned that El

Camino is not about a destination, but an inward journey, a becoming that has its own pace.

Thich Nhat Hanh often talks about "burning away our afflictions"—fear, anxieties, cravings—through mindful attentiveness. In Zen practice, we sit in full awareness, recognizing emotions and allowing them to be there. As children we often learn the opposite: to manipulate and resist our experience. In travel, I've learned first to open to my experience and to accept with equanimity what happens as a work in progress.

It is said that nature is an open secret. I learned the secrets of grapes by walking slowly through La Rioja, the grape growing region of Spain. I learned about grapes with names like *Tempranillo, Viura, Malvasia, Graciano,* and *Garnacha Blanca.* Some grapes are sweet, others pungent, some sour. I loved the strong musky fragrance of the earth as I walked along the fields, the simultaneously sweet and juicy blue-black grapes hanging in bunches. Grapes vary from the palest green to the darkest blue. Often I see life as black and white, right and wrong, bad and good. I fear making a mistake that I may regret later, whether that is a detour on the road or a work decision. This kind of thinking has limited my options and potentially kept me in a small zone of possibility. El Camino showed me that there are a thousand different perspectives, each right in its own way, each expanding possibility. I learned that there is more than one right answer. Transformation is about changing perspective, not stopping at the initial "right answer" but finding another perspective. Learning and growing is not a linear trajectory. Instead, it is more like a venturing inside, watching and waiting, and acting with faith and hope. The pilgrim falls in love with the world, seeing the extraordinary in the ordinary, with each step reframing problems into possibility. In slowing down I came to see with soft eyes, really noticing what had before been "scenery." Just as a painter learns to see and perceive form, color, texture, and structure of familiar objects, and unlearns the universal and confusing habits of seeing for information, analysis, or likeness, I was learning to see with pilgrim eyes.

Ventosa to Nájera

"*¿Quien te llama?* Peregrino, who calls you?" This is the first line of a poem written on a plastered wall on the way to Nájera. In a spiritual journey, every experience potentially has meaning. What matters most is perhaps not what can be seen with the eye, but what one feels deeply inside. I often overlook, walk around in a state of curiosity or confusion, or learn by association. In contrast, the pilgrim goes deeper, from looking to understanding, from perception to knowing and transformation. There is no need to fact-check what is happening. Life itself is its own validation.

We left the prosperous village of Navarrete, which is famous for its pottery, and climbed through almond trees to Nájera ("City Among Rocks"), passing industrial warehouses and family vegetable gardens. Nájera's architectural jewel is the fourteenth-century monastery of St. Mary the Royal. The town is built around soaring rust-colored rocks and caves and is a good place to rest and enjoy our first *paella* and *fardalejo* (marzipan). Slowing down has its rewards.

Nájera to Santa Domingo de la Calzada

El Camino is a meeting place for pilgrims. I'll stop to chat for five minutes or a pilgrim will join us walking for five hours. In the end, I say goodbye, knowing that I will likely never see the person again. It's a paradox: I feel anonymous, yet strongly connected to the fellow pilgrims. I'm learning to appreciate and to savor these encounters no matter how brief, recognizing the bond we share as travelers.

People in the countryside went about their daily chores, delivering the mail, picking up trash, buying bread. The world around me was quiet enough to hear the wind, the sound of bird wings.

We stopped at noon for goat cheese and chocolate with almonds and stamped our credentials at the deserted village of Cirueña. The cathedral in the next town, Santo Domingo de la Calzada, is probably one of the world's most unusual, containing a henhouse with a cage where a white cockerel and hen are kept in memory of a well-known miracle. The long-honored tradition begins with a story set in the fourteenth century, which tells of a miraculous event:

A family of Germans, comprising the parents and their son Hugonell, were on the pilgrimage to Santiago de Compostela when they stayed at Santo Domingo de la Calzada. The innkeeper's daughter fell in love with the boy, who rejected her. Furious, the girl put a silver cup in the young man's bag and accused him of stealing it. The judge had him hanged. His parents, before continuing on their pilgrimage, went to take leave of their son who was hanging on the gallows. Hugonell spoke to them and assured them that St. Dominic was holding him up. The parents looked for the judge, whom they found dining, and told him what had happened. The judge mocked them saying that the hanged man was no more alive than the roast chicken on his table, whereupon the bird flew up, her feathers grew, and she began to cackle. The young man was taken down from the gallows and allowed to continue his journey to Santiago de Compostela.

Santo Domingo de la Calzada to Burgos

The vineyards of La Rioja open out to plains and high-cut grass waiting to be stacked and sold. We entered the Castile region, a place of immense plains, little tree cover, and tones of ochre. This is the great *meseta* (plateau) bounded by the

Cantabrian Mountains to the north, the Iberian Mountains to the east, the Central Mountains to the south, and León to the west. There is no place to hide from the sun here. The Way of St. James traverses the north of Castile through the provinces of Burgos and Palencia. It crosses flatlands, keeping the Cantabrian Mountains at a distance.

Succumbing to the pressure of not enough days, we boarded a public bus for the forty-five-minute ride to Burgos. Traveling by bus to avoid the *meseta*, the hot and dry plains, I felt like an imposter, a pilgrim in disguise as I glanced out the window, passing pilgrims loaded down with water bottles, jackets and sneakers hanging from their packs, along the ancient road. In the Middle Ages, pilgrimage by proxy was common. "Palmers" were surrogates paid to make pilgrimages for rich clients. I mulled over the questions: *What do I do to escape or avoid the monotony of the daily grind? Is this pilgrimage really about that? When the going gets rough, or boring, or uncomfortable, where do I find hope?*

The Burgos cathedral is a magnificent Gothic monument and a UNESCO World Heritage site. Construction began in 1221 by order of King Ferdinand III and Mauricio, the bishop of Burgos. It is one of the most sumptuous and beautiful cathedrals in Spain. I was heady from the sight of angels and archangels, sepulchers, gold crosses, extravagant figures, slender twin towers, and the nave which contained the final resting place of El Cid and his wife. There are chalices of gold encrusted with emeralds, paintings of the Virgin Mary with child feeding at her breast, and a magnificent Flemish painting of Mary Magdalene.

At the St. Mary's Bridge in Burgos, old men strolled along collecting fallen chestnuts from city trees, while little girls fed pigeons in the town's main plaza. This is pure Spain. Lunch was garlic soup served in a deep bowl with a fresh egg broken into the indentation at the bottom. The *paella* for lunch was

filled with crayfish, scallops, baby clams, mussels, and shr
After lunch, we boarded the bus again to Fromista, a sedate village of pre-Roman origins. The bus, circa 1975, hummed along
in shades of burnt orange, beige, and brown, with little white
headrest covers at each seat. The sun was at its strongest as we
passed towns with names like Villasilos, Vallegera, Quintanas,
and Castrojeriz. They sounded like poetry rolling off my lips.
The ancient cottonwoods stood shoulder to shoulder, while
windmills on high ridges gazed down upon us. Cornfields to
the left and spent sunflowers to the right paved the way. We
passed a traveling circus in the town of Astudillo. A clown and
a camel brought laughter in a sea of ordinary moments.

We arrived at Fromista to the setting sun. Fromista lies on the
207 kilometer Canal de Castilla. The magnificent Romanesque
St. Martin's Church built in 1066 has rooflines of differing
angles and shapes. Our day ended in our hotel, which was
squeezed in between a cheese factory and the *albergue*. Church
bells again invited the night.

Fromista to Carrion de Los Condes

The heart carries the feet.
— Hebrew Proverb

On the road from Fromista, an old man in a red argyle
sweater, wearing a brown tam on his head, and with a wooden
leg passed us on his English, three-speed bicycle. The nearby
village of Poblacíon de Campos is a leisurely walk from
Fromista, and the local bar/grocery/post office/restaurant/
town hall is the official place to get credentials stamped. Along
the way, we met an old woman in a tattered, black sweater, navy
skirt, and torn, black canvas shoes. She told us that the village,
once prosperous when mules assisted in doing the work, has
gradually fallen into disrepair and abandonment. The mules
were replaced by tractors, which required less manpower to do

the same work. The men left for work in the cities and now the women are left alone. As we left Poblacíon, the sun and cool breeze touched red-tiled roofs. Chicory and grass competed for space on the roadside. We stopped to say a prayer of gratitude, standing in a circle at the thirteenth-century Chapel of Our Lady of Succour. We gave thanks to everyone we had met along the way, and to those who shouted, "Ultreya!"—Walk in faith and courage!

The Way continues past newly burned hay fields. Entering Villalcázar de Sirga, we came to the Church of St. Mary the White, a thirteenth-century castle fortress with an especially warm and inviting chapel, a large rosette window, and massive Roman columns that cradle the wooden doors. Five kilometers along the road past open farmland, we arrived at Carrion de los Condes. Our home for the night was the thirteenth-century St. Claire's Convent, where St. Francis of Assisi is said to have slept. The convent has a mechanical bell to invite the faithful to prayer. It sounds more like raw iron hitting steel. The attendant, a thirtyish man with wire-rimmed glasses, seemed nervous and rushed from chore-to-chore. He explained the rules of the convent in an officious voice and then showed us to our rooms. Closing my eyes, I stood in the courtyard imagining the smell of incense and the long dark robes of nuns moving about prayerfully, their hems sweeping the sandy, pebbly ground. The presence of the Holy was here in stones worn smooth by the weary and the curious, those seeking refuge from the world that waits for no one. I relished a restful night under a down comforter.

Carrion de los Condes to León

You will reach a point where
the heart tells itself what to do.

— Ajaan Chah

The sense of entering "normal" life began to creep into my consciousness. In León, people hurried with purpose and deliberation about their daily affairs. We barely had a chance to glance at the cathedral and we were back on the bus, headed to Santiago at sixty miles per hour. The landscape changed. Pine trees became mountains. Sheep grazed. Cut stone surfacing made a road through the mountains. Gorges gave way to twisted and tangled trees and red rocks. Surely, this is what the Buddha meant by the Pure Land.

I daydreamed about the foods and the taste of Spain, the taste of green olives stuffed with anchovies and fresh artichokes with cracked pepper, of soft goat cheese and aged white wine, of la quesada (yogurt pudding) and broiled trout, of bacalao with roasted peppers, of olive oil as green as grass and almond paste, of ripe figs and the palest melon with serrano ham, of crusty bread for dipping in wine and café con leche. This is Spain too.

Call me by my true name. My Buddhist roots see the close connection between myself and others, and how we share happiness and suffering. My Quaker roots encourage me to see that of God in every person. I am an elderly Spanish woman dressed in good shoes and handbag. I am the blue grapes lying in the fields of La Rioja. I am the cathedral and the churches along the Way. I am. While my heart longs to be walking El Camino, I know it is not outside me.

Through the bus window we looked at deep gorges cut into even deeper rivers. We passed fruit canning factories and grazing cows. We settled into our candied almonds and bottled water for another four hours to Santiago, arriving at last in Galicia, in northwest Spain. Galicia is separated from the rest of Spain by geography, ethnicity, language, and climate. Washed by the Cantabrian Sea to the north and the Atlantic Ocean to the northwest, Galicia is a rugged place with mountains like the Ancares and Piedrafita. It is composed of the

Galician Massif, valleys with a temperate and wet climate, inflowing water and lush, green vegetation. We passed medieval roads and fourteenth-century castles, stone crosses, haystacks, and chapels in the shade of old oak trees, and monasteries with sweet orange and olive trees. And all the while, I know the Way of St. James lies deep within me. To walk slowly across a meadow is to know that nothing of nature is commonplace. The Way of St. James invites a way of seeing, a way of hearing, a way of touching, a way of walking, and a way of being. Stolen moments of reflection are the ground of grace for the *peregrina*. Behind each moment lies the truth.

Santiago de Compostela

Santiago is full of life and energy. It is the crossroads of many worlds—Celtic and Spanish, university city and tourist trap, neat shops selling Galician lace, tapas bars, silver shops, and bakeries filled with the smell of baking chocolate and offering the Santiago torte, a flat almond cake with powdered sugar on top. *Peregrinos*, arriving from their arduous journey, mix with university students, street vendors, artists, and musicians. It is a feast for the stomach and the eyes. I savored everything: *chocolate con churros*, a decadent funnel-cake-like dessert of buttermilk fat and chocolate; ink-black calamari over white rice; crab meat stuffed in pimientos in red cream sauce; and cold salmon salad. I was caught like a spider in a web. Images of sunshine in sheltered courtyards, balconies overflowing with potted red geraniums, cobblestone streets, and the gurgle of weak fountains intoxicated me. This is a place to enjoy the stray hours.

Footsteps measure distances along the way, but the Way of St. James is not an asphalt road. The Way, El Camino, is my deepest desire to weave a strand of eternity in my own life. Long ago, before I was aware of such things, El Camino invaded my consciousness. Long ago, I was moved by the landscape, the people and the energy of this sacred Way. Nothing can prepare the *peregrino* for the experience of the Way. It is not necessary to have a staff or rucksack. It is not necessary to have a shell, the emblem of the *peregrino*. The miracle of El Camino is to walk, and by walking to become the rough cold stone, the clock tower and church bells, the grapes hanging in bunches in the vineyards waiting to be picked, the children at play on the roadside. Everything was as it should be. I listened to the church bells in Santiago, and I knew I had arrived.

Buddhist Gatha

Oh Holy One, to you who lives in the silence and stillness, in the busyness and restlessness, kindle the Light within me and in all that lives. May I go forth, walking gently on the earth and give you thanks for this journey and these lessons along the pilgrim's path. Amen. Om Shanti

Quaker Queries for Reflection

- ○ How do you travel when the going gets rough?
- ○ Where do you find God in the rushed moments?
- ○ Does the silence and stillness in Quaker meeting for worship provide a "pilgrim moment" for you?

Practice Lesson of El Camino

Next time you walk around at home or work, notice how you are walking. Feel your shoes on the floor. Become keenly aware of your surroundings. This strengthens focus on the present, sharpening awareness and mental clarity.

CHAPTER 2

Sixteen Earthly Possessions

Following Gandhi's Footsteps in India

LESSON: When you accept what you already have, you know that you have more than enough to be happy.

Eight o'clock, no later, you light the lamps.
> — Mary Oliver from her poem *The Lamps*

The time when the lamps are lighted.
> — Lucernarium, Latin

Your word is a lamp to my feet and a light to my path.
> — Psalms 119:105

Early on, I was obsessed with India and my very definite "to do" list was to see the Taj Mahal and the Ganges River. In 1990, I took a first step on that list and traveled to the city of Varanasi, one of the seven holy cities of North India. In Hindu culture, there is a strong belief that the divine is more accessible at certain places, giving rise to a sacred geography of the land itself. Partly driven by my mother's early death, I promised myself that I would "see the world." This obsession propelled me with a single-mindedness. I was afraid that if I slackened my resolve I'd succumb to fear and all my plans would slip through my fingers.

I felt like a mess caught between the longing to see and experience India and fear of the unknown. I came with a bad attitude, sporting cowboy boots, a black leather jacket, and Levi jeans as I exited the plane at Indira Gandhi Airport in the sweltering 95-degree heat of New Delhi. I knew no one.

On my first morning in Varanasi, I rose before dawn and in the chalky, blue-black light, I walked down to the *ghants*, large steps at the edge of the Ganges River. Varanasi is the place where, according to Hindu tradition, one seeks to be cremated, committing one's ashes to the river. Believers, beggars, *sadhus* (holy men), tourists, and just the curious also come to wash away their sins in the forgiving waters of the Ganges. They come to the holy river Ganges, throwing water toward the rising sun as a gesture of refreshing the soul of their deceased ancestors. Flat-bottomed rafts rest gently on the river illuminated by little boats made of banana leaves, each bearing a lighted candle in the grainy pre-dawn light. Half awake, half asleep I found myself with a crowd at the banks of the Ganges. A full bodied, wide-open rush of electricity passed through the bottom of my feet to the top of my head. The holiness of the place left me stunned as I stood in the thick moist soil, more liquid than solid. I faced the sun with a deep and new interest as it sprouted over the horizon—a miraculous mystery, the circle of night becoming day.

The image of the lamplighter on the river, lighting an old brass lantern, now stays with me on each pilgrimage. The traveler's lamp is a metaphor for the light that shines from the wisdom of travelers who have walked before us, and the light that pours from our heart. While references to "light" are commonplace in hymns, prayers, and worship, light is often used in connection with mystical experiences. For Friends, the doctrine of the Light Within describes the main channel of grace that is open to us and arises out of our belief in Christ's presence. Early Friends spoke of waiting for direction of the Light in all "temporal" as well as spiritual concerns. Isaac Penington, an early Friend, spoke of divine, spiritual and supernatural Light in all men. Thomas R. Kelly, in *A Testament of Devotion*, speaks of the "Inner Light, the Inward Christ" as not a "mere doctrine" but as the "Living Center of Reference," the "source of action," the "locus of commitment for Christians and non-Christians." Accepting that we all have access to the Light, "then it is only by joining together the bits of Light that are given to me with those that are given to others that I can begin to see the whole."

In lighting the lamp of my own innate curiosity, wonder, and awe, I engage the sacred act of awakening, remembering, and seeing. The lamp light of my own natural curiosity shines bright. The Buddha at his death said, "Be a lamp unto yourself." Quakers, in acknowledging the Light of God, refer to "standing still in the Light" as the basis of individual peace and peace within society. As a pilgrim, I have put down the tools of every-day life to be in the Eternal Light, to discover holy places, and to take the winding road to meaning.

This pilgrimage to India, like so many journeys, began with a holy longing, a search for meaning and intention, a deeper quest, and an impulse to touch what is true and vital in me. I longed to stand at the places where Mohandas Gandhi stood, to see and to be touched by these holy places and to know and understand his teachings on *satya* (truthfulness) and *ahimsa* (nonviolence). I wanted to walk the same roads in South India too where Gandhi walked in Chennai, Mumbai, and Madurai, to experience the spiritual power of these places made lumi-nous by prayer, reflection, and right action.

It is the sacredness of the yearning that distinguishes the pilgrim from the mere tourist. The longing is like a knock on the door. It is is the voice of the traveler's soul.

Pilgrimage can be a fantasy of idyllic insulation from the busyness and cares of everyday life, about escaping life's messiness or the constancy of social media. Like dreams of the good life, a fully funded 401K account and lifetime medical care, we may long for a pilgrimage journey as an escape from worldly laments. In that journey we never get lost or miss a train, and the weather is always perfect.

As a Zen practitioner, I know what it is to be entangled by longing, which leads to attachment and cravings, which are a part of the human experience. Buddhists describe this craving as the Hungry Ghost, a character with pinhole mouth, skinny throat, and distended belly. The Hungry Ghost has an insatiable appetite and is never satisfied. At times I find myself between two extremes, total attachment and total indifference. I have unrealistic expectations about how travel should be and often get angry when the trip does not meet my expectations— a set-up for disappointment.

Sometimes I travel with little planning, expecting little and getting little out of the experience, or getting a lot. The all-that-I'd-hoped-for mentality gives way to the reality of the road, moving from what could be to what is. When I make the leap from planning a trip to actually living it, things may not work quite as I had planned. My missionary zeal to see the Taj Mahal is tempered by hoards of other people with the same idea. It takes acceptance and patience to make peace with the forces of chaos and the laws of motion, to move from the simple, predictable routines back home to the juggling act of pilgrimage travel. An important lesson of pilgrimage travel lies in the strength to surrender to what is, instead of clinging to what could or should be. Arriving hungry and late at a *refugio* on El Camino, all other options long closed, the lady innkeeper served a free dinner of bread, soup, wine, and fruit—enough to take the edge off but not nearly satisfying. By showing up sincerely, wholeheartedly to what is, I've learned to trust my deepest inner intelligence, tapping into a wellspring that overflows within me. Quietly and without much fanfare, I close the gap between the life I have and the life I want. I give up an exhausting struggle to mold reality to my will and enter the slipstream of acceptance—cool refreshing waters, even when this means sleeping in one room with forty pilgrims snoring on mattresses and bunks, their steamy, wet clothes draped around heaters. Life takes on a quality of integration: wholeness arises naturally from a sense of acceptance, tolerance, and faith that whatever happens is what I want. The effort and struggle gives way to contentment, a component of peace. At its core, this is about faith, not as an abstract concept but in the conscious self-surrender to what is.

My task as a pilgrim is to be wide-awake to experience. Alan Watts, the late Buddhist teacher, has noted that we usually don't look, we overlook. Seeing requires that I slow down, to listen, to ask: "What have I seen?" "What have I felt?" "What have I touched?" Pilgrimage is not like watching a documentary. It's a first-hand encounter, like crossing a high stream, balancing my rucksack over my head to avoid walking an extra mile and a half to take a detour.

When I arrive at a new place, the first thing I like to do is look around, to take it all in with my senses, to be aware internally of how a place affects me inside and how I am affected by what I see, hear, and smell. Arriving in this way is an act of making friends with uncertainty, the unfamiliar, and with myself.

The pilgrim's challenge is to take a leap of faith to embrace cross-cultural connections with a quality of neighborliness, knowing that all people share common human conditions: sickness, love and loss, old age and death. The pilgrim risks that, in touching people and places, she may take unexpected turns and sidesteps, cultivating a flexible mind and open heart. On El Camino when I reached the top of Alto del Perdon tired and hungry, I was greeted by a Brit in a camper van selling coffee and biscuits for one Euro. He was at the right place at the right time, and I danced with glee. There was no need to ask questions, just to be grateful that he was there and had what I needed.

Traveling implies change, taking me to mountains, oceans, deserts, towns, cities, villages, woodlands and farmlands, the known and the unknown. While travel can spawn a burst of renewed energy, it can also be demanding. The journey requires strenuous and often unwelcomed adjustments: cancelled flights, lost baggage, rude taxi drivers, and wrong directions. Losing my way is part of stepping into the unknown and very different from the predictability of a pre-packaged tour. Traveling solo takes guts or, better yet, youthful fearlessness. Sometimes conditions (snow, rain, fog) are impossible to predict. Even when I miss my stop on a train, I end up learning a bit more about attentiveness and the kindness of strangers.

While pilgrimages can be done solo, in this journey I organized and led thirty seekers from America and Canada—retired ministers and lay people—to bear witness to the people of South India after the devastating tsunami in December 2004. My commitment to spearheading this journey came also as a result of a deep desire to share my love of India with other Westerners. Like many travelers to India, I came with a "love-hate" relationship, seeking to escape the rat race of Western culture for the daily devotion of ashram life. I came with great curiosity, having dabbled in Hindu culture and as a teacher and student of Kundalini yoga. I came to gaze upon images made holy by centuries of prayer, to sit under the bodhi tree, rediscover the scent of fragrant incense and the chime-chime of tiny hand bells. I had to get over being simultaneously stunned, curious, and repulsed by the rambunctious flow of everyday Indian street life: cows roaming the street to graze on gutter garbage, beggars—many of them lamed or deformed—and heat and crowds everywhere. Frustration, defiance, and resistance were part of this pilgrim's journey. On difficult days, when the smells of curry and auto rickshaws' exhaust collide with my senses, it may be best to just brood, to let the darkness be healing, to accept it and be grateful for the temporary hardship, to use obstacles to strengthen my courage.

Buddhists have a practice of praying for a requisite number of hardships, which is said to build a compassionate heart and a mind oriented toward love, knowing that hardships can serve as a furnace for transformation. It is at these times of utter conflict that mindfulness becomes especially useful: to be with discomforts, dislikes, annoyances, and strain, just as they are; to be with moments of ecstatic flow and rapture just as they are without grasping, clinging, avoiding, or detaching is the practice of mindfulness—to be with the moment-to-moment unfolding of life.

As a Quaker, I recommit to the power of Love in my inward life and outward actions. This is the power of the Inner Light, which is continually self-revealing, bringing me back from forgetfulness.

Right Sharing of World Resources

My continued affection for India and its people led me to suggest a pilgrimage jointly sponsored by the Quaker organization Right Sharing of World Resources (RSWR) and Kirkridge Retreat and Study Center in Bangor, Pennsylvania. Some members of the Kirkridge Board of Trustees were skeptical when I presented the proposal. But my faith in the beauty and mystery of India and the desire to share it with others gave me the confidence to offer the proposal, which the Board endorsed. Shortly after Kirkridge began advertising the pilgrimage to India, *The New York Times* featured a cover story in its travel section that closely mirrored my proposed itinerary. The trip was fully subscribed within weeks.

In Chennai and Madurai, we connected with ordinary people in their ordinary and extraordinary lives. We visited the micro-credit lending projects in the rural villages of Tamil Nadu, among the poorest regions of South India. We went to the lush coastal area of Kerala to visit the ashram of Amritanandamayi Devi, the Hugging Mother, an internationally revered guru.

My fellow pilgrims, ministers, retired teachers, therapists, many Quakers, and others, were all affiliated with Kirkridge or RSWR. They could have traveled to India in many ways, doing the "tourist trap" thing—taking an elephant ride in a tourist town or being bused from one silk and carpet shop to the next. Instead, they chose to explore Gandhi's legacy, up close and off the beaten track.

Mumbai (Bombay)

Mumbai is an island facing the Arabian Sea, connected by bridges to the mainland of India. Its name is derived from the goddess Mumba, worshipped by the early settlers. As part of the Indian government's efforts to reclaim its heritage and re-emerge from its colonial past, many popular monuments and streets were re-named from British to Hindu terms in the mid-1990s. Reminders of the British past—the Gateway of India Arch, the ornate Victoria Terminus, the Prince of Wales Museum, and Crawford Market—still punctuate the city. Mumbai was designed by Sir Gilbert Scott, and at times resembles a fifteenth-century Italian masterpiece dropped into the middle of an Indian metropolis. Many of the grand edifices are marred by street vendors selling everything from ladies panties to fresh coconut juice. Here there is evidence that the British attempt to stamp order and discipline on the people backfired. What remains is a heady mix of established and makeshift shrines festooned with marigold and rose petals, and seedy elegant Victorian structures crumbling under the weight of a population of more than sixteen million people. The highlights of our overnight stay in Mumbai included the Jain Temple and Gandhi's residence.

Mumbai's religious population is split 70 percent Hindu, 20 percent Muslim and a mix of Buddhists, Sikhs, Parse, and Jains.

While they are a small part of Mumbai's religious diversity, the Jains have a thriving spiritual community and are an economic powerhouse of the city. We arrived at the Jain temple to a festive atmosphere, with music and the scent of sandalwood and cow dung in the air. Altars were laden with fresh coconut, banana leaf, and marigolds. My job as our group of thirty entered the temple was to "guard" the shoes left just outside the temple doors and gate.

Temple gates are no ordinary place. This is where the spiritual and material worlds meet and sometimes collide—a thin place. It is a place to be in the presence of the Holy, to be among seekers chanting, bowing, and praying, to bear witness to those seeking rites of repentance and divination, and to observe the traditional offerings of incense, flowers, and money. I stood at the Jain temple gates, invisible and forgotten, watching the unfolding of life: the homeless, the saintly, the grief stricken, and the serene.

Squatting in a tiny crowded corner, I focused on those entering and leaving the temple, engrossed by the frantic bustle of the spiritual seekers and the dealers, vendors selling cones of incense, candles, and candy outside the temple gates. Feeling an awkward and unsettled sense of oneness with the seekers and the dealers, I saw the seeker and the dealer in me. The seeker in me was continuously leaning forward, always looking for "more," pushing hard to get ahead. The dealer in me was continually looking back, ready to cut and run, continuously doubting my true gifts.

Gandhi's Footsteps: Mani Bhavan

Mani Bhavan, the former residence of Mohandas Gandhi, is a small oasis of tranquility in Mumbai. You hear the birds well before you see the house shaded by trees, now a small museum containing Gandhi's few possessions, set in the middle of this bustling city.

Gandhi said, "Inner oneness pervades all life." This sense of harmony was present the moment I entered Gandhi's modest home. His room, the centerpiece of the house, was spare, containing few items: a small cot, a table and lamp. Perhaps it was the birds or canopied trees that seemed to envelope the house, or the intensely peaceful feeling of the place despite the constant flow of visitors from around the world.

I was reminded of Gandhi's life of struggle: the boycotts, the fasts, the civil disobedience, and his practice of *ahimsa*—of doing no harm. The simplicity of his life touched me most deeply, a reminder of my Quaker faith and practice. Simple living isn't simple anymore. I spend a lot of time with electronic devices (high-speed internet, cell phones, and computers) and may even be dependent on them. Staying up until 2 a.m. many nights to read and respond to emails, feeling tired and washed out, I knew I was ready for change. There in Gandhi's tree-canopied house, I knew that his work to bring dignity and freedom to all people was the calling of every person, and my deepest work. I saw how I was chained to the daily grind, carving out a livelihood that was no longer meaningful. At that moment, I vowed to change things.

The uncertainty of the road helped me look at my priorities: how I planned and where I placed my energy. I was learning to let go of this fast-forward pace, to wean myself off the Blackberry habit, the pressure to constantly stay in contact. Gandhi's legacy of simple living is cause to celebrate the very ordinary—writing letters, sewing, and caring for the land.

At his death, Gandhi is said to have owned only sixteen possessions:

○ 1 robe

- ⭕ 1 string of mala beads for prayer
- ⭕ 1 pair of sandals
- ⭕ 1 blanket
- ⭕ 1 pen
- ⭕ 1 bent safety pin
- ⭕ 1 metal bowl to pour water
- ⭕ 1 fork and knife
- ⭕ 1 bowl
- ⭕ 1 spoon
- ⭕ 1 lantern
- ⭕ 1 water bottle
- ⭕ 1 cloth napkin
- ⭕ 1 length of rope
- ⭕ 1 ink well
- ⭕ 1 spinning wheel

Living simply is a radical act. It means making conscious choices about precious resources, about stewardship of local and world resources, about right consumption and right sharing. This lesson, learned nearly halfway around the world, is not about rejecting modernity but about radically challenging consumption patterns. In a world made dull by mindless consumption, Gandhi's legacy points the way to a lifestyle that honors individual and collective self-sufficiency. It points to a social vision of alleviating suffering caused by social structures of poverty and racism.

Balancing Gandhi's legacy and notions of Quaker simplicity back home in a middle-class lifestyle, I know that this means more than developing "financial intelligence." Looking deeper at the spiritual core of simplicity, I realize that my spending and acquiring habits are more about a social statement than a fulfillment of a perceived need. The path to simplicity is, like many things, a path that involves awareness, right livelihood, and contentment. Standing in Gandhi's living room, with his meager possessions around me, I became aware again of the birds outside. I was happy. I accepted my fears and doubts and the unfinished business. I accepted everything. I was overflowing with fullness. I learned an important lesson: when I accept what I have, I know that I have more than enough to be happy. The simple life becomes a life of overwhelming abundance.

Gandhi's practice of *ahimsa*, harmlessness or nonviolence, continued throughout his life, as he "experimented with the Truth" (*satyagraha*), which led him to self-purification through fasting, prayer, and self-restraint (*brahmacharya*). Truth, according to Gandhi, could not be reached without nonviolence: "No cooperation with evil, civil disobedience that breaks unjust laws, standing for unpopular truth, laying down one's life for the oppressed and forgotten."[5] Nonviolence is the "soil in which the seeds of love, truth, and peace spring to life."[6]

There are real connections between the Quaker teaching on nonviolence and Gandhi's practice of *ahimsa*. As a Friend, I have trained myself to remember to act and respond in peace, to relax and feel peaceful inside. This inner peace is derived in part from my effort, faulty at best. This training has taken years of remembering and questioning. Over time there was a deep restructuring of my beliefs, of the hardened rules that over decades gained primacy, beliefs like: there is only so much to go around, help yourself first, don't ask for too much, fight for what you want. There is another kind of peace, the peace that comes without asking or wanting. This peace comes from my deepest being. Suddenly, it is there, like the sound that emerges from silence. This kind of peace arises organically from having

5 Richard Deats, *Mahatma Gandhi, Nonviolent Liberator* (Hyde Park, NY: New City Press, 2005), p. 37.

6 *Ibid.*

created, nurtured, and practiced the deep self-suggestion of peace. The pilgrim's path is to remember to walk in peace, to live with deep remembrance of peace. Travel has taught me that I live in the now. That is where I find God's presence. The pilgrim's path may be uncertain—ever changing. The day will bring its own unique revelations; my challenge is to respond in love, in compassion, and to choose wisely.

Kanchipuram

Chennai, India's fourth largest city with more than six million people and the capital of the state of Tamil Nadu, faces the Bay of Bengal on the east coast of the Indian subcontinent. It is home to a diverse religious community, including the Theosophical Society, San Thome Cathedral (a Roman Catholic church built in 1504 and said to contain the remains of St. Thomas the Apostle),and Luz Church, a Portuguese church built in the sixteenth century—the oldest in Chennai and dedicated to Our Lady of Light

Our focus in the Chennai area was a visit to Kanchipuram, the Golden City and silk-weaving temple town, containing 125 shrines dating to the Cholas and Pallavas period of 200 B.C. Kanchipuram is one of seven sacred cities of India. The others are Ayodhya, Haridwar, Varanasi, Mathura, Ujjain, and Dwarka, all located in North India and each dedicated to a Hindu deity. Kanchipuram is unique in that it contains many temples dedicated to Shiva, the agent of death and destruction, and many dedicated to Vishnu, the preserver and sustainer of cosmic order and the redeemer of humanity. Kanchi (as it is called) shares with Madurai and Varanasi the significance of being one of three cities in India where the goddess Shakti is worshipped.

We received blessings from priests at the temples we visited, including the Kamakshi Amman Temple, dedicated to the goddess Parvati, who accedes to all requests. I felt embarrassed and self-conscious as I sat before the temple priest in his orange robes, my negative "self-talk" standing between me and his blessing. After a while though, I realized that his blessing was not about honoring me, but honoring my devotion to God and to the pilgrimage journey. I reminded myself that I began this pilgrimage with little more than a love of India and the desire to share that with others. Swami Satchidananda, the great yoga teacher, said, "A real pilgrimage is when you go with nothing in hand, totally depending on God."

From the side of one of the great temple pillars, soaked with the prayers and stained with the smoke of rosewood and myrrh, I watched as members of our pilgrim group moved among the temple *sadhus*—holy men dressed in dhoti, or loincloth, their faces streaked with rice flour and turmeric. I took it all in, the lingam shrines, children running barefoot on the silky, gray soil, an old woman who squatted and squinted back at us Westerners with our clean clothes and generous goodwill. Blurring the line between *sadhus* and pilgrim, the sheer weight of centuries of prayer and devotion leveled all differences. We were united.

Mahabalipuram

In Mahabalipuram, a stone-carving center of thirteen thousand people on the Bay of Bengal, I witnessed first hand the tragedy and devastation of the tsunami of December 2004. Stunned by the people left homeless by this disaster, many in our group were brought to tears. Others said a silent prayer. Still others turned away, unable to look at the devastation, gazing instead down the beach at the few remaining coconut trees. I stared open-mouthed, looking for the orphanage home on the beach that I had visited just a few months earlier, wondering: Where are the children? Where are Mansur, Appu, and

Chandran? Squinting against the late afternoon sun, I turned and looked back down the beach to the Shore Temple, untouched. I stood there for what felt like a long time until one of my fellow pilgrims took me by the hand to leave.

Pondicherry

Pondicherry, a former French colony on the east coast, today has a population of eighty thousand. The city provided our first glimpse of ashram life. We visited the ashram established in 1926 by Sri Aurobindo in collaboration with a Frenchwoman known as the Mother. Sri Aurobindo is revered throughout India for his writings on integral yoga and meditation. He was a revolutionary for the cause of Indian liberation.

The flower-draped *samadhi* (tomb) of both Aurobindo and the Mother lies under a frangipani tree in a central courtyard of the ashram. It is a place of deep silence and meditation despite the night noise of auto rickshaws, bicycles, and heavy diesel trucks on cobblestone streets. I took my seat on the concrete floor next to a young woman whose thickly braided hair perfumed the night with sprays of jasmine flowers. The women wore saris in a kaleidoscope of colors: fuchsia, lime, peach, hot pink, May apple green, burgundy, and burnt orange tinged with crimson. Sitting on the warm concrete, I felt dowdy and unglamorous next to all this femininity, enveloped in yards of fine silk and gold bangles, gently chiming. *Did my dreadlocks and dark skin separate me from the woman beside me? Did my dark skin give me special closeness with the Untouchable caste? Did my years of yoga and meditation give me a connection to India's rich spiritual tapestry?* In the dusky twilight, with the smell of ocean breeze and petroleum, this was the perfect moment. I was just where I needed to be, full of unanswered questions.

Outside the city the red clay village of Auroville, a community set among cashew groves, was founded by the Mother as "an experiment in international living where people could live in peace and progressive harmony above all creeds, politics, and division." Opened in 1968, Auroville was designed by the architect, Roger Anger. Its centerpiece is the Matrimandir, a meditation chamber lined with white marble that contains one of the world's largest crystals. Rays from the sun are beamed into the crystal from a tracking mirror located on the roof. A sense of peace, stewardship of the land, and universal love pervades the entire community. The words of the Mother, Aurobindo's spiritual companion, resonate with me:

> You carry with you, around you, in you, the atmosphere created by your actions, and if what you do is beautiful, good and harmonious, your atmosphere is beautiful, good and harmonious. . . . Concentrate exclusively on what you want to be.

I have been addicted to beauty for as long as I can remember, drawn to beauty in all its forms. A longing mixed with sadness came over me. I daydreamed about giving it all up, occupying a shack with a thatched roof set among cashew trees, surrounding myself with uninterrupted beauty.

We take our chances. We build dreams in the blowing wind. We hold fast to our plans, but not too tightly. We endure setbacks. And then one day, we are touched by great beauty, or a random act of generosity, like finding a nest of robin's eggs still warm. We follow this beauty, this calling, and it may carry us like a strong current out beyond the moorings of doubt and hesitation. Sometimes in pilgrimage travel or in life, we find the paradise we thought we lost. We actually get what we need and change happens, like bringing fresh flowers in a room in the dead of winter. I dreamed of a life of Karma yoga: selfless service and walking the red clay soil of Auroville, my sandals and hair taking on the color of deep cinnamon. And then, in the next moment, my American impatience and expectation arose, waiting for stragglers to arrive back at the bus. I laugh out loud at my irritability and crankiness. This was a short stay in paradise.

Madurai

You pray until the prayer becomes like honey in your mouth.

— Egyptian/Coptic Prayer

The centerpiece of our pilgrimage was a series of visits to local community projects supported by RSWR in Madurai, a city of over one million people. The projects are run largely by Dalit women of the Untouchable caste, among the lowest social classes in India. Madurai, called the Honey City because Lord Shiva bestowed his sweet blessing on it, is an ancient city that was recorded in Greek documents as early as the fourth century B.C. The heart of the city is the Meenakshi Temple, a riotously baroque example of Dravidian architecture, carved with a breathtaking profusion of multicolored images of gods, goddesses, animals, and mythical figures. The temple bustles with over ten thousand visitors daily. Pilgrims come from throughout India as they have for centuries, following their spiritual longing. The air is musky, heavy with the weight of ritual, and soon I found myself clapping and swaying with worshippers in a small sub-temple dedicated to Shiva. I stared into the yellowed eyes of an elderly guru, seeing that of God in him. He stared back, a sort of benediction, tucking his orange *lungi* around his long matchstick legs, blessing me with his eyes. I blessed him back.

Yogic and other spiritual traditions hold that the true purpose of human life is to become aligned with the subtle force of grace, goodwill and trust, and to channel this energy into the physical world. It is the energy underlying every action. My challenge as a traveler is to align to grace in the blissful and knotty moments. Finding grace when I'm contracted—feeling small and irritable, even angry—strengthens a spiritual muscle: my tenderness and kindness. I struggled with a meager knowledge of this ancient place and its rituals. In the end, simply immersing myself in the swift current of devotion, I learned about pure joy and grace that come unexpectedly. I passed over a border from observer to become a witness and participant of devotion.

I connected with Gandhi's legacy in Madurai, as it was here that he first wore the loincloth and entered the Meenakshi Temple with Untouchables, a radical act at the time. We visited the Gandhi Memorial Museum and saw the bloodstained loincloth he wore at his death. I moved my lips, but no sound came out. Like being trapped in an airless, windowless room, my chest tightened in despair at the loss of so great a life. *What if, I thought, he had avoided the bullet that day? How different would our world be? Would I be different?*

In India, despite its high-tech, modern leanings, I am constantly reminded of the caste system. The tendency in human nature to discriminate against people because of their skin color, social standing, or birth, and to consider one racial group superior to another is probably as old as humankind itself. Racism was alive and well in ancient India in the Buddha's lifetime too, where pale-skinned, Indo-European Brahmins placed themselves at the pinnacle of a caste system that included nobles, merchants, workers, and priests.

As a black woman with dreadlocks, I relate closely with those on the lower end of the caste system, having lived a lifetime of overt and covert discrimination. This became clear one night returning to our hotel. As I passed by a large outdoor grill, I heard a noise from inside it, the sound of heavy steel-on-steel. As I looked closer, a man emerged from underneath the weight of the grill, covered with soot and grime. His job was to clean the grill's metal intestines. He stopped, looked at me and, seeing my blackness, he then popped a betel nut in his right jaw. Smiling, his teeth and lips stained the color of red raspberry wine, we said nothing. He dug into his pocket and pulled out a ragged tissue, outstretching his hands, fingers embedded with grime. He opened his palm slowly to reveal a stash of betel nuts. I looked into his yellowed eyes, his teeth now the color of rhubarb pie, and realized to refuse his offering would be rude and deeply insulting. I smiled and reached out my hand.

RSWR Community Projects

We traded our large coach for four minivans to enter the small narrow dirt roads of local villages of Madurai. RSWR seeks to enhance self-sufficiency for people in South India particularly Tamil Nadu, as well as in Latin America and Africa. The focus of RSWR's work in India is with women and specifically the Dalit community, the Untouchables, in micro-credit lending ventures and community development. RSWR partners work with local community projects to encourage group and individual accountability to become financially sustainable, overcome poverty, become environmentally aware, and honor individual and collective strength and community. These projects embody the communal spirit and legacy of Gandhi's life and work. He did not spend his life solely striving to end British rule; he worked to build a nation "fit for nationhood." He helped promote rising social status among the lowest outcasts of society through education, spinning, nutrition, and public health—continually identifying with the poor.[7]

We visited the Slum Women Enterprises, organized by the Society for Tribal Development in Pallam, Madurai; a Dalit women's project; an orphanage home in the village of Narasinghampatti; and an organic farm and kitchen garden in the village of Manaviduthi. We witnessed the strength, dignity,

---

[7] Deats, p. 80.

determination, and pride of women who successfully managed micro-credit lending plans, raised dairy animals, maintained organic farms, taught in rural villages, or manufactured Indian spices.

The lessons of right sharing were brought home through Bhagoda, a young woman and one of sixteen members of the four-year-old Rising Moon Self-Help Group; Pushpam, another woman who turned from conventional to organic gardening; and Numisa, who raised dairy animals. Bhagoda, a widow with two-year-old twins, earned her livelihood as a seamstress. The daily wage in the mountains where she lived was $1.00 to $1.75, an income insufficient to feed her family. She bought a sewing machine with a micro-loan from the self-help group. Her self-employment allowed her to save money and to be at home to care for her children.

Since her childhood, Pushpam's family had made their livelihood from agriculture. But the sustained drought in Tamil Nadu had driven many people to sell their land and seek daily wage work in the city at $1.00 for a ten-to-eleven-hour day. Pushpam, uses pig waste in her compost, and chickens feed in the garden on insects and compost. She also found that eggplant seedlings could begin to bear fruit faster by adding the waste and removing some of the seedlings' leaves at fifteen days.

Many landless women compost leaves and dung that they collect from common lands. Aruna, another landless woman, mixed cow urine with her neighbor's kitchen waste and bitter leaves to fertilize young plants. Her kitchen garden provided income of twelve to fifteen dollars monthly. When people asked her why her vegetables, limes, pomegranates, and papaya taste so much better than many others, she said they are organic, which encouraged others to adopt her method of gardening.

Numisa was a member of the Women Empowerment and Development Trust in the Pudukottai district of Tamil Nadu.

She received a RSWR loan of $240 to be repaid at 3 percent interest. She was trained in animal husbandry and learned how to grow fodder trees and to produce by-products from milk. The milk she produced sold at $0.20 per liter with an expected yield of 10 liters per day. Women of this cooperative earn $75 per month and incur $15 per month in expenses, netting $60 in income per month.

These women are living examples of Gandhi's call for self-sufficiency. They stand together in solidarity, affirming the real-life value of community, training, and education to improve their lives and the lives of their families.

They survive and thrive in a culture where girls are often perceived as a burden, requiring dowry. They stand apart from the global economy, which maximizes shareholder profit at the expense of indigenous people. They call us into a deeper understanding of stewardship of the land.

Tekkady

Traveling by bus into the state of Kerala, crossing the spectacular Western Ghats to Periyar Wildlife Sanctuary, we passed makeshift towns that sprang up around temples, and ramshackle tea and sweet stalls tucked under tiny eaves. The Western Ghats is a place of mossy green rice paddies, where goats graze on leftover melon rinds and discarded plastic water bottles. Blue-horned cows saunter down narrow lanes as old people with eyes soft as wet sand look on. It is a multi-generational place where faces weathered with experience keep a watchful eye, and spindly bent-over women shuffle home to prepare the day's cooked meal. The practiced curiosity of people was matched by the small sweet grin of the children. Women sauntered by in saris the color of cinnabar flecked with gold, their foreheads streaked with rice flour interrupted by a dash of ochre and red *bindis*.

We approached the Cardamom Hills, driving first through rice paddies, rubber and tea plantations, and finally into the hills of spice plantations. The smells of freshly made bricks, cow dung, and firewood drying after a heavy rain mixed in the air with jasmine, red roses, and lemon.

The city of Tekkady is full of sensations, savoring the smell and texture of spices, especially cardamom and black pepper (the queen and king of spices), lemongrass, sandalwood, holy basil, ginger, and giant yellow bamboo.

Sri Mata Amritanandamayi Devi Mission

A highlight of the pilgrimage was a stay at Amritapuri Ashram which we approached by water. Our houseboat, a *ketuvalam*, or traditional rice barge, was the main mode of transporting cargo and spices before the advent of motor vehicles. Easing through the backwater lagoons, intersecting canals, and narrow strips of land made dense by coconut palms, we entered rural Keralian life and listened to the melodic language spoken in this part of India—*Malayalam*.

I awakened to an apricot-hued sky streaked with pink rising above coconut palms. It is a love-lazy day, much as it was the day before and the day before that. The fishermen cast their net into the sea—the net falls like broken glass upon the water, disappearing into the light. The bodies of the dragonfly, mostly eyes, hover drunken-like above the water and then dart sharply, attracted to the perfumed scent of a mango tree. People go about their daily chores in their gabled and thatched-roofed houses. The *ketuvalam* approached Chinese fishing nets that rose out of the water like giant crab claws. The sweet scent of heavy rain clung to the riverbank for most of the day. Darkness folded in around me, the moonlight reflecting through my portal window.

Amritapuri Ashram is the place where devotees of Sri Amritanandamayi Devi (Amma) live or visit. Born in 1953 to a poor fishing family in the same village where the ashram is located, as a young child Amma felt the presence of God. She deeply empathized with the pain of others and sought to comfort them, giving them her own food and clothing. By the time she was in her twenties, thousands of people came each day to be comforted by her. Today, Amma, the Hugging Mother, is one of the world's most influential spiritual leaders and travels throughout the world much of the year. Her charitable initiatives include building schools, hospitals, and housing for the poor.

Long before the *ketuvalam* pulls up to the dock, the ashram emerges out of the reeds and water like a huge pink box, an apartment-like complex of perhaps seven stories, set amid dense coconut groves. The sign at the entrance to the ashram reads, Sri Mata Amritanandamayi Devi Mission. Several figures in white flowing robes float toward me, their limbs moving in slow motion to greet our group.

In our short stay, we absorbed just a taste of ashram life. We slept on plastic mattresses, on concrete floors, showered with cold water, ate simple ashram meals, sat in meditation, talked with devotees from around the world, and experienced an early morning *puja* (fire ceremony).

The next morning the entire ashram was scurrying, excited that Amma would be leading *kirtan* (devotional chanting) and then giving *darshan* (blessings) to the devotees. Her white-clad disciples spent most of the day sweeping, cleaning, and readying the meditation hall for Amma's arrival. That night, I took my place with hundreds of others at the front of the meditation hall as Amma entered to the sound of the *tabala* and *tambore*. The response of her followers was electric. Amma blessed us and swayed with spiritual ecstasy to the mantra, *Om Mani Padme Om*, as we continued to chant in unison until the wee hours of night. I found myself dancing with my head swaying just slightly from right to left, my body erect. Reaching within for the softness of the rhythm, I danced off beat to the *tabala*. The music was coming from inside me. I savored this offbeat, slow motion, quiet, and unhurried dance—so unlike me. I felt connected to the crowd of believers, but also connected to my own offbeat rhythm. That night I got a glimpse of being set free from the rush and hurry. I accepted my own, secret music stronger than the *tabala*. My dance became an expression of freedom and liberation of spirit. For one transformative night, I surrendered to the power of devotional chant. I gave myself over with hundreds of others to just the music, just the chant. My eyes are blind and my ears are deaf to everything except love.

> *May the tree of our life be firmly rooted in the soil of love. Let good deeds be the leaves on that tree; May words of kindness form its flowers; May peace be its fruits. Let us grow and unfold as one family, united in love.*
>
> — Amma

Quaker Queries for Reflection

- ○ What does Gandhi's teaching on simplicity mean to you?
- ○ How do you practice *ahimsa* in your daily life?
- ○ What truth is waiting to emerge in you today?

Practice Lesson of India

Keep a gratitude journal. Become aware of the treasures of life: your measure of health, your family, your work. Begin or end each day by recalling one or more gifts of abundance. Gratitude expands the heart and brings us more alive in the moment.

CHAPTER 3

Iona

Pilgrimage to a "Thin Place"

LESSON: Look back to see how far you've come.

Set up road markers for yourself;
make yourself guideposts;
Consider well the highway;
the road by which you went.

— Jeremiah 31:21

Quaker-Buddhist Roots

I undertook this pilgrimage to reconnect to my Christian heritage. It had been years since I left the Catholic Church. While I found comfort in the Catholic rituals, I was an unbeliever. Perhaps I was looking for a faith to match my beliefs. For me, the Kingdom of God is not waiting for us after death. It lies in the beauty, vastness, and diversity of life lived daily.

I became acquainted with the Religious Society of Friends (Quakers) through a woman I met at a retreat in New Mexico. I have a special fondness for the Santa Fe-Taos area, having worked as a farmhand at Ghost Ranch, a 21,000-acre tract of red canyons and mesas set not far from the village of Abiquiu, where Georgia O'Keeffe lived and worked. At Ghost Ranch I met Doris, a Quaker and fellow spiritual seeker, who recently moved to the ranch from Pendle Hill, a Quaker retreat center and intentional community outside Philadelphia. Doris had a pivotal impact on my spiritual maturation. She encouraged me to investigate Quakerism, especially since my home in Pennsylvania was situated within a stone's throw of half a dozen Quaker meetinghouses.

I was immediately drawn to the basic facets of Quakerism: the belief in a direct and unmediated relationship with God, the Inward Light. This Light, from the Quaker perspective, is within each person at birth, overcoming our separation and our differences, leading to an awareness of the needs of others, and a sense of responsibility toward them. I resonated with Quaker meeting for worship, connecting with the silence and the simplicity of the meetinghouse. Quaker meetinghouses vary: they could be a three-hundred-year-old building or a room in the local public library used for that purpose. Generally, they all have stark simplicity in common: there are no religious symbols, no statues, no altar, no pulpit, nothing that would serve to distract worshippers from coming into the presence of God. Meeting for worship is an hour of stillness, usually on Sunday mornings. It is a time of inward prayer, contemplation, and reflection. Anyone who feels moved to speak may do so, speaking from personal experience. This is called vocal ministry. In the silence, simplicity, and stillness of Quaker meeting, worshippers begin to feel more settled or gathered, and often speak of experiencing a quality of peace, of God's presence. Vocal ministry is not a function of an individual, such as a priest, but is a gift of grace available to all people. At the end of the hour, the worshippers shake hands and the meeting comes to an end.[8]

Quaker testimonies—guides to faith and practice, such as equality, simplicity, nonviolence, integrity, and community—felt familiar and intuitive to me, like good *karma*. My travels through Asia, South America, Africa, the Middle East and Europe had broadened my view of the diversity of religious tra-

[8] Harvey Gillman, *A Light that is Shining, An Introduction to the Quakers* (London: Britain Yearly Meeting, 2003–2005), p. 29.

ditions and cultures. My Buddhist roots began with travel to Asia and continued with study and practice with Thich Nhat Hanh. In 2003, I was ordained by Nhat Hanh as a lay member in the Tiep Hien Order (Order of Interbeing). As I entered these diverse cultures, my goal was no longer simply traveling, but mutual understanding and recognition of the values we share, strengthening my Quaker belief in the basic goodness of all people.

Quakers and others are turning to Buddhism for practical solutions to everyday problems in worship and in life. At its heart, Buddhism is a practical religion, stressing the value of self-exploration and testing the parameters of these teachings by one's own life experience. Quakers, like others, face real challenges in opening to God's presence. I am often lost in a sea of distracting thoughts, which are particularly problematic during silent worship. I tend to intellectualize feelings. In other words, my mind tends to get in the way of coming closer to the Light within me and others.

Increasingly, I have seen many people from many religious traditions look to the 2500-year-old wisdom and traditions of Buddhism. Buddhist meditation and the practice of mindfulness develop focused concentration and deep awareness in daily life. Mindfulness brings full awareness to ordinary, everyday activities. This practice can enliven and deepen my capacity to open to the Light Within by stabilizing my awareness and concentration, leading to greater clarity of mind. This type of awareness and clarity goes well beyond the *zafu*. In travel, and especially pilgrimage, I have a rare opportunity to do soul work: to find my inner voice, to find a place where I meet God. This discovery has a way of expanding the heart that flowers naturally, organically into care for others—compassion.

Buddhist meditation develops moment-to-moment awareness. One learns to focus on "just this breath," resting in the fullness of the present moment. This focus takes me out of my head and into my heart, from doing to being. I am permitted just to be. This became clear on a trip several years ago to Plum Village in the south of France to visit Nhat Hanh's monastery for Tet (Vietnamese New Year's) celebrations in February. As I walked the nearly abandoned landscape around the tiny French hamlet of Dieulivol, I was near turmoil about my never-enough-time work life. I was scared about how to continue to work and continue to find time for a deeper sense of meaning in life. As I walked, I became aware of a feeling deep, deep inside me, an untouchable core, a precious core, a sanctum that insulated me from fear and from happiness. The feeling, burning like a bonfire, was steady and dependable. This was my center. This was the present moment.

Quakers, like many others, are continually striving for balance, and even efforts to simplify our lives through the Quaker testimonies may be complex, fraught with perplexing choices. In Buddhist meditation I am balancing my energies on a deep level—calmness with alertness, for example. The ability to hold divergent feelings and sensations in awareness clarifies my discernment process.

Some Quakers have been greatly influenced by Buddhist books and magazines, which have grown exponentially in the United States. For example, Thich Nhat Hanh's book, *The Miracle of Mindfulness*, has sold more than 125,000 copies since its 1975 publication, and his later book, *Being Peace*, has sold at least twice that since its first publication in 1988. Some Quakers dabble in Buddhist teachings, reading the occasional article. Others delve deeply into Buddhist books, and still others may join a *sangha* (Buddhist community), undertake regular meditation practice, or attend retreats with a qualified teacher.

At first glance, it may appear that Buddhism and Quakerism have little in common. After all, Buddhists do not believe in God or recognize the salvation of Jesus Christ or the Holy Spirit. However, a closer look can be revealing. The Quaker belief of that of God in every person has long opened Friends to worship with other faiths. Buddhist meditation and Christian prayer share common elements. Prayer strives in part for inner concentration and self-reflection. Self-reflection and self-discipline are desirable in any religion, and recognizing this commonality provides a meeting ground. The Buddhist practice of *metta* or loving kindness meditation, in which we extend friendship, goodwill, compassion, sympathetic joy, and equanimity for ourselves and all livings beings, touches very closely on ideas of Christian prayer, in which we cultivate receptivity and the capacity for forgiveness, kindness, and love for ourselves and others. The ability to meet people 'where they are at'; the ability to extend friendship, even to strangers; and goodwill are all essential tools in the pilgrim's rucksack.

On a trip to the White Mountains, hiking the rugged trail from Greenleaf to Galehead Huts, I was so exhausted and hungry that upon reaching a false peak, I threw my backpack down the side of the mountain. It was waiting for me when I climbed down the trail of overgrown roots, rocks, and alpine flowers. Arriving at the hut late for dinner, I scrambled into the hikers' dining room to find a place at one of the rock maple tables sticky with laminate. Surveying the place, the food seemed nearly gone. I felt the soft rush of disappointment under my heart. Just then a member of the hut crew approached me with a steaming plate of lasagna and broccoli. I put a wedge of vegetable lasagna in my mouth, and then another. I chewed and swallowed, washing down the cheese and tomato sauce, the crunchiness of broccoli with cold mountain water. I ate with vigor, my hiking boots still on, laced up to my ankles, my red bandana still soaking wet. I ate for all those who have gone to bed hungry. I ate for those sleeping on the trail that night. I ate for all those with a hunger that food would not satisfy. I learned about the kindness of strangers and the bonds we shared as strangers together on the road.

Quakers have a special link with Thich Nhat Hanh. In 1967, a small group of Quakers calling themselves AQAG (A Quaker Action Group) sailed to Vietnam during the war to deliver medical relief. This action was possible in part because of the existing contact between these Friends and Thich Nhat Hanh. The effort blossomed into an ongoing relationship between activist Friends and Buddhist monks and nuns "engaged" with struggles for justice, which in turn helped to form the International Network of Engaged Buddhists.

Buddhist meditation has strongly attracted Quakers who engage in silent meeting for worship. The practice of meditation harmonizes with silent meeting for worship. In meeting, waiting with silent expectation on God, opening to God's loving presence which is always available, is similar to the meditational practice of creating a spacious and receptive mind that is fertile ground for peace, equanimity, openness, and balance. Quaker-Buddhist meditation courses are periodically offered at Friends events.[9]

Buddhists and Quaker share a familiarity with the depths of silence and stillness. As Friends, we may have experienced a deep sense of community in silent meeting for worship. We feel "gathered" in the common bond of silence and faith. Words seem extraneous at these times, and the atmosphere is permeated with unity, goodwill, and peace. Similarly, for Buddhists, silence is often seen as a prerequisite for entering meditation. Buddhist meditation stills the body and mind. I cultivate a spacious heart, a heart that accepts all, without trying to change or fix things to suit my tastes. This acceptance is the foundation of mindfulness and feels ancient.

The Quaker peace testimony, grounded partly in the conviction that there is that of God in each person, roughly equates

[9] Events include workshops at the annual Friends General Conference Gathering; at Pendle Hill, a Quaker retreat center in Wallingford, Pennsylvania; and at Woolman Hill, a Quaker retreat center in Deerfield, Massachusetts.

with the Buddha's teaching on love. In the Dhammapada, the Buddha teaches that hate never dispels hate. Only love dispels hate. As a Friend, I understand that using my capacity for love and goodness achieves more than threats or punishment. I do not ignore evil, but I recognize that harming those who harm me doesn't solve any problems. This isn't easy. Some days I'd much rather get real satisfaction from pulverizing the bully from junior high school than see her in her baggy sweatpants as a fundamentally good and decent person. It takes effort at times, a lot of effort.

As I grow deeper in my capacity to accept things as they are, I feel greater balance and equanimity—not leaning forward into the future or clinging to the past, but centered to receive the present—renewed and strengthened. I've learned an important lesson about the nature of impermanence, a fundamental concept of Buddhist philosophy—accepting change and uncertainty should be done one step at a time. The traveler lives in a state of impermanence, moving from one place to the next, one vista to the next. Along the road I meet a stranger. We chat for awhile and then we part. Sometimes we exchange addresses, but often these connections are fleeting. Sometimes I may stay for a brief overnight at a quiet village or decide to stay for two days. Traveling and uncertainty are two sides of the same coin. This uncertainty is balanced with a fair measure of purposefulness and direction that give meaning to life and to travel. This is a good reminder of Lewis Carroll's words in *Alice in Wonderland*—"If you don't know where you are going, any road will get you there." I arrive at a new place and, as self-conscious as I may feel, I go out for a brief walk or go to a nearby café—just to get more familiar, to take in the flavor of the place.

Following the call of faith—whether it is to travel, work, or form relationships—is to trust the energy that courses through me. It means being willing to let life live through me and stand firm in what is already here, to be courageous enough to say, "Whatever happens is what I want," and mean it.

Iona—a "Thin Place"

My heart was knotted around a failed marriage and a string of broken relationships that cut deep into me like a river cuts into a mountainside. I came to Iona with a seeker's heart and adventurous soul, eyes wide open to God's unfolding love.

Iona is an island in the Inner Hebrides of Scotland off the southwest tip of the Island of Mull. It is only three miles long and one-and-a-half miles wide. Before the Christian era, Iona was considered a place of spiritual significance, having over three hundred sacred standing stones. In 563 A.D., leaving Ireland because he was persecuted, St. Columba sailed in a wooden boat and landed on the island. He climbed to the highest point and looking back could not see his beloved Ireland. He settled on Iona, founded a Celtic monastery, and for thirty-four years shepherded Christianity to Scotland. Iona maintained a strong independence from the Roman Catholic Church for two hundred years, and Celtic spirituality flourished in this rare and unspoiled tiny island.

In Celtic spirituality, the immediacy of God is present in all created life. The light of God is within all beings, and prayer is a celebration of the goodness of creation. Iona is said to be a "thin place," where the separation of the spiritual and the material, the seen and the unseen, is very narrow. Here, the spiritual and material worlds intertwine. Rather than seeing human nature as sinful, Celtic spirituality celebrates the inherent and essential goodness of humanity. The lessons of this ancient spirituality were carried on by the Reverend George MacLeod, who in modern times is credited with restoring the abbey church founded by Columba and establishing the Iona Community, an ecumenical Christian community committed to seeking new ways of living the Gospel in today's world, embracing peace and social justice. Today Iona remains a place of ecumenical community, a place of pilgrimage, where people of many Christian traditions celebrate the Word of God, where diverse stories come together in community to share prayer, play, and work. Pilgrims come to Iona to experience the nearness of God in the material world.

Iona is an icon for the presence of God in every place. In the Celtic tradition, prayer occurs throughout the day—upon the rising of the moon, at the kindling of the fire, at the birth of a child, at the washing of one's face. Everything is touched in grace with prayer, and in this way the mundane becomes sacred.

It's a full day's journey to get to Iona from Glasgow by coach, train, bus, and ferry. Iona is a place where time is suspended, endless. It is a place where new spring lambs have grazed for centuries and where winding roads lead to no place in particular. It is a place to be warmly greeted by the local farmer and to watch the sunset softly in the night sky. God is here not just in the Episcopalian tradition of nightly vespers, the liturgy, or in the abbey church, but in the gentle rain, the sea grasses, and the ocean tide.

Fellow Pilgrims

I came to Iona with a group of fellow pilgrims from Kirkridge Retreat and Study Center. Many were retired ministers, active clergy, psychotherapists and college professors. These were grown-ups with lived-in faces, relaxed breasts, and worn backs. As the only person of color and one of the youngest participants in the group of about thirty, I initially felt isolated, lacking a common bond and language. I stood in judgment, critical of the group that appeared too old and too white. I struggled with the part of me that wanted to be nonjudgmental and accepting, and the part of me that said that my traveling companions were different, other. The softening of my heart began when I stopped and really listened to a woman engineer who lived in Micronesia, constructing bamboo homes for Vietnamese boat people, another woman who visited Dharamshala to meet the Dalai Lama, and a woman who shaved her head and sold her belongings to build a small house on a lake with her partner. In a bump-in-the-road moment, their shared stories helped me release the grip of judgment and enter the field of acceptance. The divisions I saw so clearly faded like dimming light as these rich stories and these authentic lives unfolded.

Glasgow, the Friendly City

The pilgrimage began with my arrival in Glasgow, a city in the throes of remaking itself from its past reputation of grit, grime, and graffiti into a hip, vibrant city of stained-glass cathedrals and Art Nouveau buildings by Scottish architect and designer Charles Rennie Mackintosh. It is a unique blend of friendliness, urban chaos, and energy. The St. Mungo Museum, named for the patron saint of Glasgow, depicts the worlds' religions through art. Carvings of Shiva stand beside paintings of a traditional Jewish Sabbath. Nigerian ancestral screens are placed next to stained-glass windows of the Virgin Mary and child. The museum pays homage to the fragility of interfaith relations and calls for world harmony and mutual understanding. It gives a sense of Glasgow's openness, acceptance, and friendliness to all people, which at first took me by surprise. I had braced myself for a somewhat uptight white European atmosphere, but instead I was welcomed with a sense of oneness, even by strangers.

Travel to the island of Iona is complex, even from Glasgow, requiring a full day on buses and boats. On my first night in Iona, I listened to the lambs, the night insects, and the silence.

Returning from evening vespers in the stone chapel of the Bishop's House, I walked back to my small hotel to the sound of Scottish music floating from the town hall. Peeking through an open door, I saw a black man dance a jig with a white woman. An elderly woman danced with a small boy. Two girls danced together. I was drawn in by the music and joined in the dance, throwing myself into the music, swirling and turning with delight, laughing with glee. I let go into the lure of the music and laughter. The day's end had arrived and I had learned an important traveler's lesson—leave room to be surprised by life.

The Iona Pilgrimage and St. Martin's Cross

For centuries, millions of pilgrims have come to Iona seeking healing, inspiration, and new beginnings. The day-long walking pilgrimage around the island to places of historical and religious significance is simultaneously an outward journey and an inward journey of reflection. We began at St. Martin's Cross, named after the fourth-century Roman soldier who in sharing his clothing with a poor man received a vision of Christ. After his baptism he became known for his conscientious objection to serving in the Roman army, and later, as the Bishop of Tours, he played an important role in the mission to the Celts. The cross contains the Celtic everlasting pattern of the weaving vine, which represents the interweaving of heaven and earth.

I anticipated the spiritual energy of Iona. I read about it. I daydreamed about it. What I did not plan for were the sounds of Iona—or, rather, the quiet of Iona. The quiet is impressive. It penetrates every part of me. It creates a kind of space to hear clearly, even very mundane sounds, like the rustle of the wind penetrating leaves, the drizzle that hits the soft roof, the neighborly greeting from across the fence. My city mind, filled with too much thinking, was thrown at odds with the deep stretches of quiet. By listening I hear the gaps of pure presence between the sound of the wind and the cold rain against windowpanes. This unfamiliar quiet sometimes felt awkward to me, like a loose-fitting dress. I wanted to fill the silent spaces—play a radio, read, talk to someone. This discomfort hung around until, with gratitude, I realized that it arose from simply "being" with nothing to do. *So this is what it means to "just be."*

The Augustinian Nunnery

The remains of the thirteenth-century Augustinian nunnery, built about the same time as the Benedictine abbey, stood at the heart of the local community. At the center of town, the small primary school, village hall, and clinic surrounded what remains of the abbey. I closed my eyes and imagined life here, the nuns walking about the chapter house, cloister, or refectory. We know very little about them. The ruins stood as a faithful reminder of women's ministry, often a forgotten place when history is written.

"In Memories' Garden, It is Always Summer, 1973." These words are inscribed on the tall oak bench just off the sacristy. In this cloistered courtyard among the crumbling walls, a sheltered perennial garden stood of blue indigo, chartreuse ladies mantle, pink columbine, blood-red peonies, and yellow St. Johns wort—a living tribute to those who are forever laid to rest.

Gardening and the Marble Quarry

The ocean polishes translucent marble, "Columba's Tears." Workers quarry the southeast corner of the island for marble— translucent serpentine streaked with green. The marble was used to build the communion table and baptismal font of the abbey church. The marble quarry reminds me of the earth's evolution over hundreds of millions of years, of my place in creation's history, and my responsibility to care for the earth.

This responsibility gets played out in my garden. It is the place where spirit meets spirit and where I feel whole.

Gardening was not second nature to me, growing up in Brooklyn. A large sycamore tree, the only one on my street, fascinated me. I recall summer days when I stood with the tip of my nose nearly against it, examining its mottled bark, thinking it was both strange and lovely. Now through gardening (particularly growing garlic) I've learned to slow down and to notice the raw truth of the moment: the way the wind blows and the sun's direction over the garden, when to harvest the curly end of garlic scapes and how to carefully work and loosen the soil around each bulb, feeling the roots shift free. I garden because I can't live without it, because I feel a covenant with the land. My Quaker faith invigorates my sense of land stewardship, and my Buddhist roots instill a quality of interconnectedness.

My spiritual awakening to the land began long before I arrived at Iona. It started when I worked as a farmhand on the 21,000 acre high desert research farm at Ghost Ranch, a Presbyterian retreat center and once home of the painter Georgia O'Keeffe, in Abiquiu, New Mexico. The ranch is another thin place, where the material and the spiritual worlds seem to come together. I came to the ranch for the first time in the summer of 1978 while in college. I tooled around on the back of my boyfriend's motorcycle, exploring this brand new world. Immediately and urgently, I fell in love with the landscape—the mesas, mountains, desert—and felt myself drawn back again and again. This time it was the late summer, early fall garden season. I was in my late thirties with little more than a hankering to get the dusty red soil underneath my fingernails. I came with a metropolitan body. I came with a screaming inside my skull, seeking renewal in the natural world.

I planted sixty pounds of garlic, one clove at a time in the shadow of Pedernal, a mesa or flat-topped mountain, which

O'Keeffe painted over and over again. Everything I learned about farming and food on the ranch, I learned from Judy, a feisty sixtyish woman, sun bleached and tough as boot spurs. In addition to being an expert farmer, she was an amateur potter, making shallow, azure colored bowls. She baked Indian corn bread from scratch on the rusted cast iron pot-bellied stove in the corner of the farm's adobe hut, where we stayed warm on chilly mornings and took shelter from the sun on brutally hot afternoons. Eventually, she left the ranch to make a film with her son, traveling to the high mountains of Mexico to capture the monarch butterfly migration. I weeded cilantro in between the long rows of garlic, learned how to grind blue corn into a fine flour with a hand grinder, and washed lamb fleece after shearing until it was oily and silky to the touch. I discovered heirloom tomatoes, squash, corn, pumpkins, and beans, and learned to save seeds of heirloom beans.

Eventually, we are asked "Who are we?" "What matters?" "Why?" On the ranch I began to ask these big questions about my relationship to the land, to farming and feeding myself and others. Once I opened the door to these questions, there was no turning back. I began to examine my consumption patterns, which before I had taken for granted. Water is a precious resource on the farm, and I noticed how I used water in my daily life. The soil, mainly rock-hard clay, requires loving care to cultivate the top layers for planting. I became aware of the use of organic fertilizers to support the soil.

On the ranch I came to understand the interconnection between caring for the land and the taste and quality of the food we harvested, between eating and well-being, and between what I ate and how I felt. I began to recognize the connection of growing food, caring for the land, and eating. Thich Nhat Hanh, the Zen Buddhist monk, speaks of this type of interconnection as "interbeing," a mutuality that penetrates all things. The organic gardener, for Nhat Hanh, sees the rose in the table scraps, which then get turned back into the garden, which nourishes the soil and lends vitality to another planting, which then nourishes us. In accepting the wisdom of interbeing, we touch a deep reality: life is unique, precious, impermanent, and unrepeatable.

Gandhi said, "To forget how to tend the soil is to forget ourselves." When we are in nature, we begin to remember what we are made of. We realize that not a single moment in nature is ever repeated. This is the beginning of the Quaker testimony of stewardship of the land, of the appreciation and gratitude that support our spiritual practice and enliven daily life. We can learn a lot from nature. We learn stability and solidity from the trees, fluidity from the water, freedom from the birds, beauty from a rose.

St. Columba's Bay

Our walking pilgrimage of the island took us to St. Columba's Bay, a pebbled beach at the southern tip of the island where Columba is said to have arrived from Ireland on Pentecost Sunday in the year 563. It is a place of leaving behind the past and of coming to new beginnings.

I am standing on the edge of a new beginning. Looking back, I see nearly two decades of a job that has paid the bills and provided me with a measure of safety and financial security. I see clearly what has happened. More than being wedded to a career, I am wedded to the security of a regular paycheck, to adequate health insurance, and to the dream of a fully funded retirement. I realized that what I believed and how I oriented my life—my work, time, energy and money—were two separate things. I contemplated a loving and healing God, but I placed my faith in the security of work. I valued the power of pilgrimage to discover sacred meaning in the ordinary act of travel, and yet I was impatient wanting to weigh and measure my spiritual growth. The true alignment of my heart, my stated convictions, and my beliefs were at odds with my lived faith.

Was I ready to release this measure of security, to take up the next thing, even though the thought of leaving my day job made me fearful, powerless, and vulnerable, as though my entire life force were contained in the job description? On that pebbled beach, I realized that faith, even to a place that is yet undefined, leads me back to my center. This is not about my effort or an abstract concept of faith, but surrendering to an Ultimate Reality. I imagined a new possibility and felt an opening of my heart—heart as the seat of thought, reason, and sensation. I know what to do.

The Machair

We continued walking to the Machair or "raised beach," the common grazing lands on the west side of the island overlooking the Bay at the Back of the Ocean. For centuries it was used as a cornfield for the Celtic monastery and later the Benedictines. The islanders also cultivated it, increasing the fertility with seaweed and hard work. Now it is used by people from throughout the island for common grazing. The Machair is a parable of sharing and cooperation.

In this communal place, I looked at the simple truth: I had told myself one story and lived another. On Iona I am reminded of my ultra-independence, living single and unattached. I cherish my independence yet want to be partnered. I fear being a burden to others and yet I crave intimacy. I refuse to allow others to help me but treasure generosity. The days I felt weak— the stomachaches, the nasty cold, the getting lost—invited me into the black bottom. *Could I adjust my dogged independence for greater intimacy? Could I go beneath the veneer of self-determination to travel not alone but as part of the community of seekers?*

The Hermit's Cell

Now only a secluded ring of stones, the Hermit's Cell is situated at the north end of the island. These stones, which may be the remains of a sheepfold, possibly also mark the site of a Celtic beehive hut. Over the centuries this has been a place of solitude and silence. Some accounts say that Columba spent time alone in prayer here, and this may have been his place of hermitage.

I am reminded that all too often—whether at Quaker meeting for worship or when I begin to sit in meditation—I fidget, I think about the state of world affairs, I grumble inwardly, or my attention fades out. I speculate, making worship or meditation subservient to my sexy thoughts. In meditation, my experience flows from attention to inattention, from remembrance to forgetfulness. Solitude and silence can be more like time to think and especially to ruminate: *What was that sound? What should I do next? My back hurts.* There it is again, that nasty, small-minded little voice, the little stinker, the part of me that comes face-to-face with nothing to do, with the faintest quiet, and no place to hide from my thoughts. The British psychiatrist R.D. Laing said, "There are three things people fear the most: death, other people, and their own minds." For me this meant never being alone with myself. At home, I always had the radio or the TV on. Traveling about, I always had at least two books in my daypack, fearful that I would have free time with nothing to do. My worst nightmare was being on a long distance flight with nothing to read.

Pilgrimage travel offers time for reflection in a way that often does not happen in daily life. It is a step on the path to conscious awareness of the unconscious forces that control our lives. Without time set aside to reflect, to take stock, to ask big questions about life's meaning and purpose, or just to be, we can miss out on what is truly meaningful and important. We can easily live adrift without intention or direction. Asking big questions points toward courageous action.

While Iona is a very special place and pilgrimage is a very special type of travel, we don't need to take ourselves away to any place special to ask big questions or to come into God's abiding presence. All we need to do is be attentive.

Dun I

Dun I, the "Hill of Iona," is the highest point on the island at 332 feet above sea level. On a good day, you can see the tiny islands of Cull, Tiree, Ulva, and Rum, forged of fire and ice, rock, wind and water. The biblical tradition often presents mountains and hills as places of new vision and transformation, and presents the sea, especially, as a place of risk that can suddenly and unpredictably blow into storm.

Traveling, it is easy to miss the details: the tiny flowers pushing through cracks in the sidewalks; the way the sunlight passes through the car windows; the sound of the crackle of ice, or snow falling. On Iona, I become more and more aware of everything—the stones, the hills, and the water.

On Dun I, I stopped for a breather and learned about the deeper meaning of courage. Traveling had been about forging ahead, facing my fears and stepping into the unknown with persistence and self-determination, which left little room for anything else and actually was not about courage at all. The striving forward was my way of making myself heard and seen, my way of trying to control my life's goals, meaning, and purpose. I realized that courage in its deeper meaning is not just about persistence, though this is useful, but about love. To act with courage means to face uncertainty, risk, and fear and still take action, not out of relentless independence, but from my soft center, from that place where deep promises are made and kept, from the place where great resistance and fear reside side by side. Paradoxically, this is both inviting and terrifying. What I think I know now will change with courage to act, with the commitment to faithfulness. Courage translates faith into action that is visible, graspable, tangible.

St. Oran's Chapel

We continued walking to St. Oran's Chapel, by the main gate of the abbey grounds, the island's graveyard. It is the oldest building on Iona, built in the twelfth century. Oran lived six centuries before, and tradition remembers him as the first Columban monk to die and be buried on Iona. The area became known as Reilig Oran or graveyard of Oran. Many Scottish and Irish kings are said to have been buried here. We pray that through the self-giving and deaths of Oran and Columba and the countless generations of women and men who have gone before us that we may be granted the strength and vision to continue on our journey.

In the Celtic calendar, December 22 is known as the "Nameless Day," an extra day featured in many folk tales. On this day the King of Waning Year was dead and the new King of the Waxing Year has not yet been born. Believers fast to appease the Dark Queen so that she will permit the sun to return to the world and the cycle of the year to recommence. The Nameless Day is a reminder of many questions about how I live with the dark and the light.

Queries for Reflection at a Time of Darkness

○ How do I accept moments of darkness in my life?

○ Is this time of darkness fruitful for me?

○ Can the darkness be illuminating?

An important spiritual practice on the road and in life is holding the tension of seeming opposites, allowing for the tension to coexist with uncertainty: hope and despair, readiness and patience, love and loss, community and solitude, freedom and relationship, and on and on. When I feel pulled between opposites, I recall the teachings of Thich Nhat Hanh. I have heard him say not to be caught in dualistic and discriminative thinking. Like a multivitamin I take every day, I carve even the briefest moment in the day to remind myself of my deepest aspiration. Each day the brilliant illumination of an unexpected moment of aliveness becomes the antidote to living a right vs. wrong, dualistic mentality, and I am reminded that all there is is now, and to live this moment wholeheartedly. I am here now in this place now with these feelings now, these tensions. The beliefs tighten my jaw, the muscles around my eyes. I come back to feeling my hands and feet, hearing the neighbor's voice next door. Coming back, coming back.

The Crossroads

Stand at the crossroads, and look
and ask for the ancient paths,
Where the good way lies, and walk in it,
and find rest for your souls

— Jeremiah 6:16

On Iona, one celebrates the immediacy of God, seeing God at the heart of each moment. The *Carmina Gadelica*, the book of poems, songs, and prayers of the Celtic people handed down orally from generation to generation, is filled with examples of Jesus Christ as "Son of the Storm, of the Wind." The ocean turbulence is a metaphor for the wild stirrings in my life.

We paused in the pilgrimage at the crossroads. It's the only intersection on the island, and a place to come together, to gossip perhaps. People from the North, West, South, and East meet at the crossroads to share stories about firewood that may have washed ashore or newborn lambs. I paused here to contemplate the mid-point of my life. I turned to look behind me to see the territory I had just walked. Before me the path continued leading down toward the ocean. From this perspective, I take in the landscape in a different way, with greater breadth and depth. Looking back reoriented me for what might lie ahead. I would have missed a lot had I not stopped at the crossroads to look back. Looking back is not just physically stopping to turn around, but taking time to reflect: to understand the common threads that weave in and out of my life; to be in greater attunement to my "inner teacher," that which is real and vital within me; to gain greater appreciation of people and places; to weather emotional storms. This is not about selfish introspection. Rather, it is a path of compassionate action, tapping into my deepest center.

The crossroads reminds me of the words of Robert Frost:

Two roads diverged in a wood , and I—
I took the one less traveled by,
And that has made all the difference.

— Robert Frost, *The Road Not Taken*

But how do I know which road to travel? The way is clear: In every step on every road, the traveler should take the road that leads to more love, more gratitude, more peace, and more kindness. Looking back, I soaked in the land, the water, the sky, and the people with gratitude.

Queries for Reflection at a Crossroads

As you think about crossroads in your life, ask yourself:

❍ Where is God moving in me?

❍ How has God touched me and changed me at my crossroads?

❍ What are the unanticipated gifts of life at a crossroads?

❍ What have you learned from looking back?

The Moorlands

We ended the pilgrimage at the moorlands, a place of light and water, soaked by peat bogs and sphagnum moss, embedded with wildflowers. Water is everywhere. It eddies, meanders, and whirlpools.

Paths of cotton flowers surrender their petals to the wind, while on rocky knolls saxifrage, yellow wild primroses, and buttercups lie in the dewy grass. Here, tiny daisies close tight at nightfall and in cold or wind.

For six hours and seven miles we walked from gravel road to open pasture, through meadows and peat bogs, across moorlands, scrambling up rock ledges to stony beaches, and across boulders. We crossed heather and lanes to pray in song and story, to pause, listen, and reflect. I accepted the inner turmoil, the doubt, to live the first flush of spring, at least for awhile.

The wind brushed my hair, penetrating my heart, which had grown tough as day-old bread by not enough loving and not enough laughter. The sky grew brighter and then darker and then brighter again. This pilgrimage is an invitation to inner knowing, to see with childlike eyes, and to reconnect and remember that I am made in the image of God, and this connection is deeper than any brokenness.

Comfort: The Pilgrim's Reward

Comfort has gotten a bad name in a world of work hard, play hard. An hour spent daydreaming in a nearby park doesn't count as productive use of time. I'm constantly steered away from my own inner wisdom toward something more elusive that I must hurry to find elsewhere. I have to convince myself that I deserve to rest, to take a nap at mid-day, to walk without direction. My outer knowing, outer self goads me on toward being productive. My inner knowing quiets down in the healing space of an unstructured, unplanned day.

This inner knowing doesn't come easy to me. In college, I worked at Burger King at night and attended classes during the day. In graduate school, I worked as an intern and attended classes. In law school, I attended classes by day and worked in a law firm at night. I took pride in keeping all the balls in the air. There wasn't much time for play or even to think. I kept that pace up, feeling ambitious and smug in being able to handle it all. Then I realized I was making the kind of sacrifice that one cannot easily recover: inside I was dry as dust.

The root of the word comfort means "to make strong." This pilgrimage also fortifies my body, mind and spirit for ordinary moments that go unnoticed. On Iona, I found the gift of the unhurried life. Rather than fearing that my time was not well spent, I learned the ease that comes from allowing life's unfolding.

To get to the Applecross Hotel for afternoon tea, I walked past the ferry dock, Alison Wagstaff's B&B, and the post office. The hotel, with its peach-colored walls and mint-colored cabbage rose curtains, was filled with potted red geraniums and trailing purple petunias hanging low in the sunroom facing the street. It's a homey place where visitors settle with great civility for afternoon siesta beside the charcoal fireplace in large overstuffed chairs decorated in tropical prints, or in the front parlor in black wicker rocking chairs.

I held in new esteem my nightly ritual of sleeping with a hot water bottle under a wool blanket and on down pillows. I became accustomed to breakfast of hot oatmeal or oatcakes. I grew to appreciate the necessity of a nap and afternoon tea. Long and leisurely lunches at the island hotels usually involved a bowl of wild mushroom soup or squash and coconut soup or white pearl onion and parsley soup. The bread was homemade, thick-cut with pieces of walnut and tiny sesame seeds on top. Afternoon tea always included Scottish shortbread and munchkin cake, washed down by strong peppermint tea.

Comfort is so much underrated.

Two Fields

To get to the west end common grazing lands, which led to the beach at the Back of the Bay, I passed two ordinary fields, divided by a *ha-ha*—a low stone wall of roundish boulders bleached yellow and pale white by lichen, all mossy and old—that seemed to disappear from view at a turn in the bend. The field to the right had neatly mowed grass with a diagonal path cutting across it and a perfectly straight path, running alongside the wall. The second field, its neighbor, was wild and overgrown with weedy Queen Anne's lace, wild purslane, dandelion, thistle, stinging nettles, feral rose bushes, and knee-high tasseled grass. Both paths were well worn by visitors and local folk alike who knew that this was the shortcut past the nunnery and the Iona Heritage Center and Tearoom to the abbey church, the main attractions on the island.

People of many faith traditions come here to worship at the abbey church, hopeful and expectant for some conversion from each service. Expectations are high for this small congregation, tending to the souls of many. The worship service, more like a celebration than a service, though homey and welcoming, seemed meager compared to the lusciousness of the land, the feel of place.

Two plots, side by side, one wild and one tamed are much like two competing forces in my life. The wild and untamed parts of me want to cut loose the house payments, the obligations of work, the tact to know what to say to whom and when, to be renewed, to allow the pilgrimage to lead me not just to a place of healing, but to a place of resurrection, like the free and eternal wind, to sweep my life clean. Two fields side by side, one wild, one tamed. *How do I acknowledge the wild parts of me that want to plant garlic in a high desert farm, to Mambo well, and to learn to weave from a Navajo woman?* The questions are deeper than the answers.

Village Life

The soul exists and it is built entirely out of attentiveness.

— Mary Oliver

The Honey Man

The old man who gathers heather and clover from the moorlands lives at the bottom of a rolling hill in a white stucco house trimmed in blue, weathered with age. A satellite dish is tucked gently under the eaves. From rickety stalls at the rusty front gate, he sells heather-laced honey in miniature baby food jars for one pound. He also sells white marbled stones from the marble quarry, stones he chiseled with the sign of the cross to be worn as pendants around one's neck. The front yard is overgrown with re-seeded snapdragons and daisies. Early lettuce sprouts in troughs and cement buckets smartly covered with chicken wire. Like everyone on Iona, he always keeps his front door open, and you leave your money on the front porch.

In his 1953 book *Meditations of the Heart* theologian Howard Thurman writes a parable of the desert dweller,[10] who each night leaves a lighted lantern by the roadside to cheer a weary traveler. Beside the lantern is a note with detailed instructions to his cottage, so if there is any distress, the traveler may find help. To the desert dweller, it is not important how many people pass by in the night and go on their way. It is not important who the stranger may be. What is important is that the lantern burns every night and every night there is a note, just in case. This parable reminded Thurman of a time he visited Rangoon. While there he noticed along the roadside a stone crock with water and some fruit left there by Buddhist monks to comfort and bless any passerby—a "spiritual salutation." The fact that Thurman was a traveler from a different part of the world, speaking a different language did not matter.

[10] Howard Thurman, *Meditations of the Heart*, Harper, 1953, p. 90

What mattered was that he was walking by. Iona is like the lighted lantern or the crock of cool water by the roadside—replenishment in the desert for the worn-weary, an oasis of light for the heart, mind and soul. There is vulnerability in openness and trust. What matters is to try.

Snails

The organic farm that supplies much of the vegetables for the island's two hotels is a well-cared-for place of young snow peas, spinach, tansy and lupine. The soil is crumbly, inky black and full of earthworms and ants. It lies protected by a six-foot hedge of magenta and pale pink fuchsia, growing old with woody branches and petalled flowers that fall open, dangling like drop earrings.

At night the snails come out—and rabbits! Snails creep along, moving with antennae outstretched, searching. With delicate poise, they rest halfway up the ochre-colored water iris at the side of the ditch. They live content with this pace, no bother to the lambs and cows that graze nearby. The snails, the lambs, the cows form a complicated web of life, interdependent yet separate. This is a well-ordered universe, a living example of Indra's Net, the Buddhist metaphor for the interdependence of all things. Each intersection in Indra's Net is a light-reflecting jewel, and each jewel contains another net, ad infinitum. The jewel at each intersection exists only as a reflection of all the others, yet it also exists as a separate entity to sustain the others. Each and all exist in their mutuality. Each has no existence except as a manifestation of all, the whole.

The Post Office

It's easy to fall in love with Iona; just hang around the post office, for example. The clerk parks her Royal Scottish mail bicycle up against the building. I climb the three shallow steps past the tiny flower garden of forget-me-nots, wine-colored peonies, and snow-in-summer, growing from cracks in the wall, to enter a tiny trailer-like building on a white sand beach.

The postmistress sells stamps and envelopes, clear tape, *Par Avion* labels, Herbamare seasoning for the kitchen, and Mitt's Essential Oils of clary sage, clove, and basil. There are handmade chair cushions with hand-drawn scenes of the ocean, the abbey church, or the Celtic Cross, and hand-knitted socks and sweaters from local women.

The slower I move, the more I see. I come to the fullness of my being in attentiveness to all things, no matter how small. Pausing to take it all in is a spiritual practice. I'm learning to accept the temporary nature of each moment—the view from a high hill, brief rest on a wooden bench at the side of the road, a stranger's greeting: these moments leave me simultaneously aware and strengthened by the connection. Travel encouraged me to invest more of my presence and energy in these temporary, transitory times because of the possibility they hold: the moment is here now and then gone. Through travel I invest myself fully, wholeheartedly, to see the beauty before me, even if it is brief.

Afternoon Tea

How wonderful it is to do nothing,
and then rest afterwards.
> — Spanish proverb

"It's easier to get forgiveness, than permission," said Jenny McLellan, a fiftyish handsome Scottish woman and warden of Dunrig, a Christian "quiet house." This was an offhanded comment about trying to get permission from the island officials to open a craft shop in the large shed next to the Iona Heritage Center and Tearoom. Arriving at Dunrig was yet another gentle reminder of what I never do for myself: I don't give myself permission to be nourished by such things as taking time for a cup of tea and conversation in the middle of the day, or even more radical, a nap. I'm too busy to rest. I'm too busy to slow down. I live a confident self-sufficient life, addicted to speed and the satisfaction that comes from being productive. And yet I know that this time of rest on Iona has made me more awake and alive. In the stillness my inner faculties, my way of perceiving was sharpened with rested eyes, seeing in new ways.

Going Sailing

If you want to go sailing around Iona you have to book at the first house on the left after the post office. The sign on the front door gives all the details and you leave your deposit and particulars in the McVities Premium Cookie tin. Just show up at the ferry dock at 2 p.m.; weather permitting, you sail.

I'm a city dweller, with an iPhone, a laptop, and a GPS. I live where there are stoplights and telephone poles. I've learned to travel lightly, which is not just about what I pack for a trip, but also recognizing those things that lead me away from what really matters. I'm often absorbed in keeping it all straight: weeding the garden, getting the car serviced. Traveling lightly, a lesson I learned while walking El Camino, is not just a balance of what to take and what to leave behind, but cultivating inner lightness. This means noticing and letting go of expectations, even small ones, to appreciate what is happening now. Here on Iona there are no stoplights, no billboards, just rural landscape and blue sea.

The island of Staffa, a one-hour ferry ride north of Iona, inspired the painters and was immortalized by Mendelssohn. It has the imposing Fingal's Cave, basalt rock carved by the sea, puffins, pink sea thrift growing in rocky ledges, and yellow trefoil. This uninhabited place is suspended forever in time and space.

Space for Wings

We are already what we are seeking.
Until we realize this, we will never find
peace of mind nor awaken to the totality of things.

— Christopher Titmuss

Looking up from a rocky outcropping on Dun I, at the top of the highest point on Iona, I see the space between the wings of a hooded crow. The space where bones and feathers merge in freedom and strength: to fly, to soar, to come to rest. I too need space for wings, space to take off the dusty cap and work coat and put on garments spun of gold, space to rest and play, to forgive and to be forgiven, space to wonder about my own becoming.

On my last day on Iona, the rain was like background music, steady and soothing, living waters, refreshing and healing. I envisioned this day would be like most days on this island of peat bogs and moss, at the edge of Europe, far away from everywhere and close to all that really matters.

I came to Iona full of questions without answers, longings with a hint of direction. The answer came in the worship service at the abbey church, in sharing bread of many grains with many people. The questions lay before me like the wild irises growing at the roadside and the newly born lambs.

To be received in Christ, to paraphrase the Rule of St. Benedict, one needs to let go. But what if you have a fear of high places, a fear of falling? Sometimes the questions get caught in my throat like tiny fish bones. Sometimes I want to send the questions sailing out to sea like a note posted in a bottle off a marooned island: *Will the next past-life regression therapy workshop or soul-intensive improvisation session bring me closer to God, bring me closer to my true self?*

My spiritual house has many rooms and on Iona I looked into the dusty, airless places and went down into the junk cellar and came up lighter, cleaner, and freer. Here, I relearned to trust, to give my life over to something bigger—the questions. The anxiety, mixed with anticipation, doubt, fear, hesitation, hope, and trust, all co-exist. Anything can happen.

We have been told that nature is an open secret and yet deeply mysterious, and we are urged to "live the questions." To be present to the lavender sunset, the Caledonian pine and white ash of Mull, the sea thrift nestled in lichen-blotched boulders of Staffa, and the new lambs of Iona, is to be fully alive. This pilgrimage was about living the questions, becoming who I am meant to be. The more deeply I live the questions and move toward my true self, to who I am called to be, the more deeply I become an expression of God consciousness, drawn closer, deeper in Love.

Prayer and Mindfulness

Prayer is opening into love,
opening into that radiant and centerless love
that surpasses and enfolds all of life.

— Tilden Edwards

In prayer I don't need special words or a special time. I am formed, in part, by my prayers that shape my decisions, emotions, and habits. Prayer can be what gets me out of bed in the morning. It can undergird worship, deep friendships, and even painful divisions. Prayer is dynamic, responsive, inclusive, and portable. Prayer can be done walking, standing, sitting or lying down. Prayer accompanies me wherever I am, no matter the circumstance, on the road or at home. It links me to transformation, but even before transformation, there is intimacy. Intimacy rests at the core of prayer—intimacy and awakening of my senses. Before I seek to change especially my anger, doubt, or impatience, I want to get really intimate with it, to look at it carefully, to understand it. In welcoming these less than pretty parts of myself, I regain a sense of wholeness, an appreciation of life's fullness.

Prayer, too, calls for risk and persistence. Unlike an off-the-rack suit, it requires patience, practice, and an open heart and mind. For Friends, prayer requires coming to meetings for worship mentally disarmed and vulnerable, rather than out of a sense of duty or mechanical pattern. As a traveler, my prayer has taken on a new shape. Often traveling and arriving at a new place, I settle in a hostel with strangers less than three feet from me, the rustle of backpacks being emptied and filled, background conversations, people coming and going. At these times, I learned to turn inward. If the noise in the hostel gets tiring, I seek a quiet place outside—leaning against a stone wall, sitting on steps—finding moments of space to clear my inner landscape for what is to come next.

As a Buddhist, I am touched by the prayerful practice of mindfulness. Where there is mindfulness, there is love grounded in awareness, wakefulness, and presence. I move beyond thinking to knowing and being. In such moments, I am truly awake and alive. I put aside everyday forgetfulness to come into the immediacy of the sacred, the spiritual, grace.

Often my day-to-day living is like channel surfing or going on a shopping spree. I move from event to event, battered by a tidal wave of sensation and sound. I grasp and grab, drawn in by impulse and neon lights. I know what mindlessness looks like—preoccupied with plans or memories, rushing through daily activities, breaking things because of inattention, forgetting someone's name the moment I'm told, and snacking without being aware of eating. Mindfulness—the heart of the Buddhist teachings—is intentional. My intention to create greater peace, solidity, and compassion for myself and others elevates the practice of mindfulness from a mental exercise to a sacred act.

And now back in Glasgow, I hear the distant din of traffic—taxis, cars, planes, and just outside my window a songbird closed the day. All roads lead home.

Practice Lesson of Iona

Take a daily, hourly pause practice. Be aware of how far you have already come and of your efforts. Stop, take three deep breaths through the nose, feeling the belly rise and fall. Notice how you feel. Notice what you have already accomplished. This builds awareness of the body and breath, and activates the parasympathetic nervous system, calming the body and mind, reducing stress.

CHAPTER 4

Camellias and Stone Mountains

A Spiritual Pilgrimage to Japan

LESSON: If you offer yourself to others, you will never be a stranger.

Donning my pilgrim's robes
  For the journey across the sea,
  I know it is far—
  Yet my mind cannot measure
the distant path these white clouds follow.
                    — Chōnen, *The Temple Route* (938–1016)

  "Would you tell me, please, which way I ought to go from here?"
  "That depends a good deal on where you want to get to," said the Cat.
  "I don't much care where—" said Alice.
  "Then it doesn't matter which way you go," said the Cat.
  "—so long as I get SOMEWHERE," Alice added as an explanation.
  "Oh, you're sure to do that," said the Cat, *"if you only walk long enough."*

  — Lewis Carroll, *Alice's Adventures in Wonderland*, 1865

Japan is a country teeming with mountains and temples, with 70 percent of the total land area covered in mountains and forests; the remaining 30 percent is crammed with people. This land-people relationship has kept Japanese village life still closely connected to mountains and forests that store water and produce lakes. Water flows down rivers, reaching the flat lands. Terraced rice paddies cut deep into hillsides, creating watery veins.

I came to Japan to walk the twelve-thousand-year-old traditional pilgrimage to eighty-eight temples of Shikoku in the Kii Mountain Range and to visit the island of Shodoshima. The island is dedicated to Kannon, the Bodhisattva of Great Compassion, also known as Kwan Yin or Avalokitesvara in other parts of the world. Kannon is one of the most revered figures in Buddhism, often represented as a woman who is said to absorb all the world's suffering. Kannon teaches deep benevolence of heart, mercy, that we may open our spiritual eyes in understanding to others.

The eighty-eight-temple pilgrimage of Shikoku is one the world's largest sacred zones, covering three areas—Kumano, Yoshino, and Koya. Together they make up the "sacred zone" which has been described as the esoteric triangle of Japan, considered hallowed ground, associated with Shinto Buddhism. This pilgrimage invited me to look at the world through non-Christian eyes, to meet Buddhists of differing sects—Shingon, Rinzai, Tendai, and Shinto. For years earlier, I had studied and chanted the Heart Sutra, one of Buddhism's most revered prayers on the nature of all life. My first Zen teachers were from the Rinzai Zen tradition, and part of our regular sitting meditation practice included chanting this sacred prayer in a particularly distinctive rhythm. Each time I chanted the *sutra* I flung myself totally into the rhythm, into the words. Sitting in meditation, chanting, I surrender the urge to figure the words out, to have it all clear, to understand: "Form is emptiness; emptiness is form. Form is not other than emptiness; emptiness is not other than form." Like the big sky of the New Mexico desert, vast and present, I drop the inner call to have this make sense, and instead let the words melt, flood over me. Everything is humming with life within me.

My traveling party consisted of two Americans and three Australians. We followed a circular pilgrimage route without goals in the usual sense—no holy of holies to which one journeys. What is important is to go all the way around and return to the starting point, to close the circle.

Our small group of five women, one an ordained Australian Buddhist priest, began in Osaka and took the high speed train to Mount Koya, the world headquarters of Shingon Buddhism. Mount Koya or Koya-san is situated near dense forests. A World Heritage Site, it is a place where monks, pilgrims, and tourists mingle. We started with palms joined in a prayer of safe journey at the gravesite of teacher and philosopher Kobo Daishi (774–835).

The lane from the town's main street to the temple gate is lined with pilgrim inns and shops selling incense and candles. The temple gate is flanked by menacing giant deities, glaring down at the insincere. Historically and customarily, passing through temple gates is an act of commitment to complete the journey started, even at the risk of death—strong tonic for the casual visitor. In Japan and throughout Asia, temple gates serve an important role as civic, news, and market centers. Gates leading to temples also are symbolic, suggesting a passageway between the secular and sacred, the material and spiritual worlds, a "thin place." Even the *henro's* or pilgrim's loose-fitting white jacket or *byakue* attests to this vow. White, in Japan, is the color associated with death. Written on the back of the jacket is the mantra, the haiku invoking the name of Kannon, which we would recite upon arrival at each temple: *Namu Kanzeon Bosatsu.* Entering the temple's ancient cemetery, I came to the stone ablution basin, which held water for symbolic purification. I grasped one of several bamboo dippers to rinse my mouth and a pink towel to dry my hands. Purified by water and ritual for the journey ahead, bowing deeply, I crossed the temple gate.

I walked the ancient graveyard hidden in the shadows of tall pines and deep moss, and came upon a very special section for fetuses of miscarriages and abortions. This part of the cemetery is dedicated to the deity Jizo Bodhisattva, said to aid the weak and the poor. Jizo heals illness and is regarded as a special guardian of those in difficult or dangerous transition, such as pregnant women and travelers. Jizo is particularly seen as the caretaker of infants and children who have died, including fetuses lost to miscarriage and abortion. Hundreds of Jizo statutes line the cemetery. He appears as a little man made of gray stone, and he stands on a mossy patch, his eyes closed, and his lips bear a faint smile. A fern leaf arches over his head, an umbrella holding the morning dew. He wears a small red bonnet and cape, and in his pocket, sewn in the cape, is a prayer written on a sheet of white paper, a prayer to a dead child—a prayer of love, loss, and longing. Other Jizos stand on mossy mounds, their features softened by dampness and cold. Faded flowers and a teddy bear were placed in remembrance.

The rough seas of my past, memories of my own abortions and miscarriages, came rushing back like the inflowing tide. Feelings of loss, regrets, and pain are never out of reach. I called on the spirit of Jizo to guide me, and on the spirit of Kannon, "she who hears the cries of the world," to hold me in compassion and ease the heavy artillery of loss.

In the Bible, there is the parable of the barren fig tree. In it, a man had a fig tree planted in his vineyard and when he came looking for fruit on it, he found nothing. He said to the gardener, "See here! For three years I have come looking for fruit on this fig tree, and still I find none. Cut it down! Why should it be wasting the soil?" The gardener replied, "Sir, let it alone for one more year, until I dig around it and put manure on it. If it bears fruit next year, well and good; but if not, you can cut it down." In this parable, the tree is worthless. The gardener offers to shovel manure around it with no indication that new growth will occur. Much like the fig tree, I feel fruitless, barren, from the loss of these miscarriages and abortions. *Where is God in this? I feel broken down, unable to move. I put my career ahead of motherhood and now I am paying the price for it!* Fault, blame, loss, and disappointment overwhelm any presence of God, of a sacred inner life. And yet, the parable speaks to me of waiting—holy waiting, a waiting that settled in me as a concentrated stillness—and rootedness much like the fig tree. These are times when all seems dead; my feeble efforts—like shoveling manure on a dead tree—do not yield what I had hoped. Yet there is the faintest glimmer of hope, a tiny seed of knowing that God is present, even in this. God's nearness and the harvest of hope heals even in times of unexplainable loss.

This pilgrimage is a deep plunge into Japanese culture and customs, and the pilgrim clothing is a significant and symbolic part of the experience. I left street clothes behind to adopt pilgrimage garb—white jacket and pants, pilgrimage tote with incense, prayer book, and candles. My straw hat, or *sugegasa*, stretched over my eyes, provided shade. A brass bell hung from my belt, calling me to prayer, a reminder of life's impermanence. Its sound faded quickly like a lover's quarrel, passing and transitory. Over my *byakue*, pilgrim's jacket, I wore a *kesa* around my neck. It was embroidered in gold letters of the *Hannya Shingyo*, Heart Sutra. The *sutra* is one of Buddhism's most significant texts to describe the experience of liberation gained from meditative insight. The *kesa* is usually worn by a monk, priest, or nun, but in undertaking this pilgrimage I am given the same status as a priest and permitted to wear it. My pilgrim's bag carried all the essential items for the journey—incense, candles, lighter, and a pen. These too are inscribed with a mantra—*Dogyo Ninin*, which means that although I travel singularly, I am accompanied by Kannon who always walks with me. I present my *nokyocho* or book at each temple to be inscribed with a sacred seal of vermilion and calligraphy, certifying my visit. These seals are said to contain Kannon's power of the temple, like having Kannon's personal autograph. I carried an *ofuda* or temple calling-card too. At each temple I wrote my name and a prayer on the card and deposited it in a special pilgrim's box. Finally, I took with me a pilgrim's staff and in my case a retractable walking stick that not only symbolized the heart of the pilgrimage, but served as an object of support up steep mountain paths and to steady my footing across stepping stones. At each temple, I would burn incense, light candles, and chant the Heart Sutra in Japanese, the only words I know from years of practice with my former Zen teachers.

Behind me near the ancient tomb of Kobo Daishi stood the Great Stupa of the Sacred Precinct bearing thousands of red paper lanterns crowding the ceiling's dim recesses, each flickering light a prayer and an offering. I walked to the bell tower, at first hesitantly; I bowed, then squinting through the smoky incense I pulled back the heavy timber to swing it forward, striking the bell, announcing my arrival to the temple deities and to Kobo Daishi. Making my way to the main hall, facing the *hondo* or main temple, joining my palms and bowing, I lit a candle, offered a stick of incense, and climbed the steps of the wide veranda sheltered by the projecting roof. Pigeons flew and cooed about freely, drawn by the offerings of handfuls of rice.

I chanted the Heart Sutra with such intensity that I felt suspended between this moment and the next to come. I chanted it over and over again, feeling its power and fullness. I was not chanting alone, for myself, but for all people, for the unborn children, for my ancestors, for all beings. I felt a strangeness and a strength of spirit. When I stopped, a heavy silence and softness fell upon me—a sense of wholeness, completeness. My struggle to understand Japanese culture, language, and custom yielded to a connection fused by Spirit, a harmony and deep beauty. Suddenly, a sense of love came over me. It was like being in love with the world, with everyone. The feeling took me by surprise, overcome by a sense of gratitude. The unfinished business back home, the efforts to set matters straight, the cheap hurts, frustrations, losses, and disappointments—none of this mattered in this weightless moment. There was no rushing, no hurrying, no figuring things out. I was suspended in the simplicity and complexity of being. A door opened within me and I walked through it.

Worship at temples is an individual and communal act. Some kneel devoutly. Others pray audibly. But the phrase on each pilgrim's lips is *"Bu setsu maka hannya hara mita shin gyo,"* the *"bodhisattva* of compassion doing deep understanding,"* the opening verse of the Heart Sutra. Worshippers streamed by like obedient children with their long tapered candles and stick incense, adding them to mounting flames that smoldered in urns, dusting the air with scented smoke. I felt a moment of quiet celebration, a merging and coming together for a greater good, of being received in the larger community where no one is a stranger. In these times, I learn that I am free, to lay down the heavy load, and to trust that where I am is where I need to be. The pilgrim's inward journey is as natural as breathing. Like the scent of a freshly plowed field, one cannot escape the inner life as it is already here. The pilgrim's work is looking, feeling, touching, and being.

The silence of the hall and the cemetery at Mount Koya was interrupted only by the sound of running water through deep, moss-covered channels. I walked back down to a sub-temple and residence building for monks and then back outside the temple gates. The gate that one enters is the same gate by which one returns to the world outside. Three elderly men kept warm around a hibachi in the early morning April chill. I felt changed, cleansed, and lightheaded by the promise of a new beginning.

The first step in understanding the significance of temple gates is to recognize the act of bowing as an act of prayer. My first experience with bowing came on my maiden trip to India in 1990. As I entered the plane at JFK Airport, the stewardess, wearing a long, flowing sari, in one motion looked at me, joined her palms beneath her chin, lowering her eyes as she gazed into mine. I was simultaneously stunned and stiff, half-standing, half-bowing, feeling embarrassed and awkward . Over the years, I have learned the art of bowing worldwide. In Zen Buddhism bowing, rather than being an aspect of practice, such as prayer or reverence, is practice. Bowing, done with single-minded focus, is meditation in motion. There are specific times when one should bow, such as when one enters or leaves a temple, when one greets a teacher, monk, or nun, and at certain times during the liturgy. The essence of bowing in Buddhism is joining hands together, bowing deeply, and letting go of one's small, selfish mind.

Many years ago, with my Rinzai Zen teacher, I learned the strict and formal rules of bowing: the way to hold my hands, the angle of my body, how deeply to bow. In the standing bow one begins with palms together, joined at the level of the heart, bending at the hip joint with back straight until the body makes a right angle. From my Mahayana Buddhist teacher, I learned the art of full prostration, bowing, then kneeling and putting palms up on the floor, touching my forehead to the floor, with my entire body resting face down. Bowing, whether a half bow or a full prostration, shows self-respect and an acknowledgement of one's capacity for transformation. To bow is to recognize the Buddha nature within myself and others, to recognize my capacity for meaningful change. The way one bows symbolizes intention and quality of mindfulness, turning an absent-minded movement into prayer.

It was cherry blossom time in Japan—late April, a time of great cheerfulness. People go about in groups of twos and threes and families gather together under cherry tree groves for a picnic lunch. It is a fleeting time. Cherry blossoms have an ethereal quality. They are here now, but with the slightest breeze, they are carried by the wind. Early spring is the traditional season for beginning a pilgrimage. It was a time of hiatus for farmers, a slack period before the winter wheat could be harvested and the rice seedlings transplanted in the same fields after they were flooded, plowed, and worked into hospitable mud. Today, there is no slack time. Our lives are no longer calendared by the planting seasons, but by Blackberrys, iPods, and text messaging.

Each temple of the pilgrimage was irregularly spaced. Some were in cities, others on mountaintops, still others beside valley streams or waterfalls. Walking this ancient pilgrimage route, I was aware of the legacy of those who sculptured the rice paddy fields, watered, manured, and tilled the soil. This is an ancient, fertile landscape. We passed fields of rape, grown for their delicate oil, fields purple with clover, and beds lush with tender green rice seedlings. Along sandy coasts, through farmlands, cities, jagged mountains, I know that Kobo Daishi walks alongside me. I felt the spirit, the thousand-armed Kannon, the embodiment of compassion, embracing me and the arms of Jizo protecting me.

Leaving Mount Koya, the pilgrimage took us to the remote forested hillside of the Seiganto-ji Temple, a UNESCO World Heritage cultural property and Tendai Buddhist shrine, located on Mount Nachi near the Nachi Waterfall. This temple is steeped in legend and history, situated in a place of natural beauty and revered for its healing properties. At Seiganto-ji, the legend begins with a tale.

During the reign of Emperor Nintoku (313–399) a famous priest named Ragyo Shonin ("The Naked Saint"), while traveling back to his home in India, was shipwrecked in stormy seas off the Kii Peninsula and was cast ashore on the Kumano coast.

In the dark night, he saw a stream of golden light coming from Mount Nachi and so he set out toward the mountains in order to discover the source of the mysterious light. Following the river, he ventured deeper and deeper into the mountains until he arrived at Nachi Waterfall, which was shimmering like a ribbon of light. Ragyo decided to remain there until he completed the grueling ascetic practice known as "The One Hundred Day Waterfall." Night and day he stood beneath the thundering waterfall, which severely lashed and pounded his body. On the morning of the final day, suddenly the waters parted revealing a tiny golden image of Kannon, all aglow. The image then flew toward the weary holy man and alighted on his arm. Ragyo was so profoundly moved by this experience that he installed the image in a small hermitage that he had built and worshipped Kannon until he died right there on the mountain.

After Ragyo's death no one ventured into the wilderness of Mount Nachi. Then one day during the reign of Empress Suiko (592–628), a holy man named Shobutsu Shonin had a dream. In his dream, Kannon told him to leave his home in Yamato and to travel to Kumano in search of Ragyo's golden statue of Kannon. When Shobutsu arrived at Nachi Waterfall he began ascetic practices beneath Nachi Falls, in the same manner as Ragyo had done three hundred years before. He decided that he would stay under the waterfall until he had a vision telling him where the statue was to be found. However, it was only the start of spring when Shobutsu arrived at Nachi and the water was still icy cold. After only three days and nights of practicing in severe conditions, Shobutsu lost consciousness, his body became frozen stiff, and he floated away down the river toward the ocean. Suddenly, there appeared a young boy, who waded into the water and rescued Shobutsu. "Who are you?" Shobutsu asked. But the boy just smiled a radiant smile and said that he had been sent as a messenger to warn Shobutsu that extreme ascetic practice was not the Middle Way of the Buddha. Then the boy just as suddenly disappeared and Shobutsu realized that the boy was a manifestation of Kannon. In his place, from under the ground he saw a light glowing and when he dug there he found the tiny golden statue of Kannon. Shobutsu then carved a larger than life size statue of Kannon and placed the golden image in its heart. This is the statue that is venerated to this day as the "Nachi Kannon" at Seiganto-ji Temple.

The rain slashed sideways as we traversed switchbacks and mountain passes on foot in the mist and clouds of the Kii Peninsula. The roar of the waterfall so close to the temple drowned out all other sound, and sheets of cold rain covered the mountain like a tight-fitting hat. At a break in the downpour, a completely arresting young monk stooped to sweep fallen leaves into a neat triangular pile underneath an ancient camphor tree. Winter-blooming camellias offered a splash of pink and red, their flowered petals floating in a rusty metal bowl. During the night I was awakened by the rain beating on the metal roof of the pilgrim's lodge. It was still pouring, still chilly in this mountainous land the next day as we prepared to leave.

At dawn, my four pilgrim companions and I bundled up for the trip down the mountain. I wore a turtleneck underneath the sweater, Gore-Tex® rain jacket and pants. My walking stick helped me along the path, muddy with pools and gullies of brown water formed by the rain. The downpour, however, could not dampen my buoyant spirit. Clinging to tissues, a bandana, and caramels, I made my way down the slope, which was mainly rock and rubble as the path girdled the mountain. Several hundred feet down, my breathing grew heavy, wheezing in the cold, damp morning air. We descended several hundred feet further, struggling with the mud and washed out places on the path in the early morning darkness. We reached a rocky crevice, realizing we took the wrong path. On our return, retracing our steps, a housewife from the cottage above the ridge hailed us down. She had watched our progress from her home, which was perched on the hillside. "You can't go that way. Go straight down the hillside where the path picks up again," she warned as she ran to meet us, wearing flip flops and umbrella. She had brought two big oranges: one for us and one for Kobo Daishi. *Settai*, giving to pilgrims, persists even today and cannot be refused. The old belief is that Daishi still walks the pilgrim path. It is a way for the giver to participate in the journey, a pious and meritorious endeavor. I am filled with gratitude. This moment could have passed me by easily as just another person and just another day. The pilgrim's heart grows wise with gratitude. Wisdom comes from experience, not just knowledge, but insight and discernment. The pilgrim's path is really a crash course in wisdom: knowing what is good, what to do and not to do. The wise person sees the truth of a situation. She recognizes generosity and doesn't mistake it for weakness. She sees love and doesn't mistake it for sexual desire. She sees honesty and doesn't mistake it for insult.

Kimiidera, a Shingon Buddhist temple located on Mount Kimi, sits between three natural spring wells: the Well of Purity, the Well of Good Fortune, and the Well of Willow Healing, protected by Japan's Department of Environment. Built in 1509, Sakuramon, the Cherry Blossom Gate, lies at the base of the 231 stone steps. We climbed the steps in silence, stopping at a small waterfall that feeds the water of the three wells below. Beside the waterfall was a stone engraved with a haiku by Basho:

Miagureba
Sakura Shimafute
Kimiidera

Watching these blossoms
falling, falling, I yearn for
Kimiidera's spring.

As we entered the main temple, heaped before me were strips of wood, each bearing the name of a child who died through miscarriage or abortion, in front of Mizuka Kannon, the deity of water babies. Tiny straw sandals were tied to screens around alcoves, offered by pilgrims or local people with prayers for a safe journey. We prayed here, dipping water from the stone basin and pouring it over the statues of Jizo. In washing them, we cleansed ourselves.

Kokawadera Temple, "Temple on the Ko River," a Tendai Buddhist shrine, is dedicated to the protection of children. People come to Kokawadera to pray for healing of children and for an easy birth.

Sefukuji Temple at Mount Makino lies at the crossroad of mountain passes and is known as the "Temple at the End of the Book." It is said that when the ascetic *En no Gyoja* was wandering through these mountains chanting the Lotus Sutra, this was the place he rested at the end of his long recitation. We climbed the one thousand stone steps covered with tiny ferns and moss, through dense pines and across running streams to reach the mountaintop temple. Before reaching the very top, we made two stops—first at Kobo Daishi's Shrine, the "Shrine Imbued with Love," a quaint thatched roof hut where he was tonsured as a monk in 806, and second at a miniature pilgrimage shrine. This shrine contains all Kannon images from the pilgrimage. It is said that if one cannot go on the whole pilgrimage, one can pray before these eighty-eight images and receive the same spiritual benefits. Before descending, we stopped for a bowl of green tea at the mountainside shack. The elderly couple who ran the shop spends most of the day breaking branches, stacking firewood and tending the propane fires to keep the water hot for making green tea and baked tea sweets. We sipped green tea and nibbled sweet *mochi*, welcoming moments of rest before descending the mountain's spine. I ate my sweet, a tiny lump of chewy, cherry-blossom-scented *mochi*, in five bites. I felt myself becoming part of the pilgrim's path, part of the mountain and stone steps along the way. Even the pain in my shoulder left me feeling grateful, vibrant.

Fujiidera Temple, the "Wisteria Well Temple" of Shingon Buddhism situated in the sprawling suburbs of Osaka, was wrapped in wisteria, a purple cloud in full bloom. The temple is famous for its Benten Shrine, housing Benzaiten, the Shinto patron saint of the creative arts—especially music and poetry. At Hasedera Temple, the massive, hand-carved Kannon statue made of a single piece of camphor wood was said to have been washed ashore and found by a monk who brought it back to the temple.

We visited temples dedicated to healing the sight impaired and temples known to prevent calamity from striking, as well as temples made famous by their flowering azaleas, hydrangea, and lotus. Temple paths were illuminated by moss-covered stones, translucent in the dew, and wrought iron lanterns filled with long-burning candles.

I didn't mind the cold and damp, the steep hillsides, the moss-covered stone steps that disappeared into cloudy mountaintops. It was the *sentos* (Japanese baths) that terrified me. *Sentos* are the modern equivalent of the neighborhood coffee klatch, except it is segregated by gender and everyone is naked. Nudity is taken as a matter of course, like no big deal that you are standing (or sitting around) with a few dozen women lathering and scrubbing themselves polished clean. I learned quickly that *sentos* have a bright line of etiquette. But even before I ventured down to the bath, located in the basement of the pilgrim's inn, I was prepared with a large plastic bag, a small wash towel, a pumice stone, liquid soap, and a change of clothes. The first thing was to remove my shoes, which was easy to remember because roughly two dozen other shoes were all lined up neatly at the entrance. The Japanese have a way of turning their back to a door entrance and then slipping off shoes smoothly and still backwards entering through a doorway. This may seem awkward at first, but I realized when I returned to the entry to retrieve my shoes, they would be facing in the right direction to just slip them back on and keep going.

I entered the *sento*, taking my slippers off in this backward seamless motion, feeling rather proud of myself. The small locker to stow my clothes had an artistically carved wooden key, a small work of art. Everything mattered. The attendant pointed to what appeared to be a price list on the wall. I nodded in approval and gave her five hundred *yen*. She motioned for me to walk to the right. Staring straight ahead at the locker, the time had come to remove my clothes. I thought: *They're all looking at me! I looked away from the locker. I'm right; I feel like a foreigner; I am a foreigner!* An elderly Japanese lady took me by the elbow, and bowing deeply, nodding, and shuffling, she tugged me along to an opaque sliding glass door. She slid it open as steam poured over me, sticking in little droplets to my dreadlocks. Inside, about two-dozen women—all bathing—just continued bathing. Some were on plastic stools scrubbing and brushing their whitish, translucent skin. Some women were soaking up to their necks in circular Jacuzzis. Others were wading in pools of sulfur water, and still others jumped gingerly in and out of cold baths, said to improve circulation. And yet with all this activity (commotion, really) the bath was perfectly quiet. Women sauntered from one bath to the next, soaping and rinsing under the tap water before they entered the pools. My fear melted away as I floated in a warm sulfur tub. I had prepared myself for a fight, though deep down I was frightened. I had prepared myself to be the unwelcome visitor. I told myself "someone will be nasty to me . . . I won't be treated right." I recalled Mark Twain's words in my head, "My life has been filled with terrible misfortune, most of which never happened." Watching the others, I took my small hand towel, wrung it out and used it to dry myself. A damp sheen remained all over my body, ready for scented oils. I felt like I sat in a massage chair for three hours, a little like Jello, and a lot refreshed. Again, I am reminded of my Quaker values, seeing that of God in all people, trusting their goodness. I learned a great lesson: the more I offer myself to others, the more others offer themselves to me.

Some temples are places for family outings, enjoying a picnic lunch of take-away sushi, or vendors selling roasted chestnuts and candied ginger. Some temples are set among the high mountains with vistas of gaunt trees, cloud-swept ranges and the patchwork valley below. Mountains conjure up images of wandering holy men, mountain ascetics, like Kobo Daishi, the founder of Shingon Buddhism, revered throughout Japan as the greatest pilgrim in the history of Japanese religion.

It was a cold and blustery day as we arrived back by van to Kyoto. In the heart of the city is Daishin-in, a Zen temple famous for *shojin ryori*, vegetarian temple cuisine. I closed my eyes before the temple altar, recited the Heart Sutra, feeling its subtle blessings and my elemental presence, counting my *mala* beads of rose quartz as they slipped between my fingers 108 times. Clearing my throat, the words streamed from my lips spontaneously, without interruption, like pouring oil from a jar. Standing before the image of Kannon, the Compassionate Heart, my breathing, bowing, and chanting formed one incantation.

Daishin-in, the only Zen temple on the pilgrimage, is a neighborly place where people regularly walk dogs and practice early morning *tai chi*. Austere white-washed walls come into view from the Zen garden of raked pebbles and gnarled azaleas. As I turned the corner around the side of a building, I was startled by two pink winter camellias that held their bloom in the chilly, morning air.

In the traditional sense, this walking, driving pilgrimage is a penitential journey, undertaken to cleanse body and mind, to purify the heart. Like many spiritual disciples, I am reminded to set out early and put up early, that this is a circular pilgrimage route, with no beginning and no end, no coming and no going, borrowing from the Heart Sutra. The pilgrimage path is not the means to an end. The path is the goal itself. Like the practice of meditation and mindfulness, there is no end. There is just the practice, just the path, which continually opens before me. As soon as my small mind clings to a small aspiration, the way changes, is made easier, or more difficult. With each step on the path I grow in trust, in faith.

Chado—The Way of Tea

The first cup moistens my lips and throat.
The second cup breaks my loneliness.
The third cup searches my barren entrail. But to find therein
    some five thousand volumes of odd ideographs,
The fourth cup raises a slight perspiration—all the wrong of life
    passes away through my pores.
At the fifth cup I am purified.
The sixth cup calls me to realms of immortals.
The seventh cup—ah, but I could take no more!
I only feel the breath of cool wind that rises in my sleeves....

           — Lotung, *Seven Cups of Green Tea*[11]

Crossing the Setso Inland Sea, I left behind the temple city of Kyoto and fellow pilgrims, taking the fast boat to Shikoku Island for a tea ceremony at Ritsurin Parks's teahouse—Kikugetsutei, the "Moon-scooping Cottage." The park, comprised of six ponds and thirteen miniature hills, sits against the deep greenery of Mount Shiun, reminding me of a traditional

---

[11] "Seven Cups of Green Tea," poem by Lotung, included in Okakura Kakuzo, *The Book of Tea* (Boston: Tuttle Publishing, 2000).

Japanese watercolor painting. There is deep harmony in the teahouse's varied elements: the carp- and turtle-filled pond, the azaleas and iris in bloom, the surrounding pine trees.

The practice of drinking powdered green tea was brought to Japan by monks returning from their studies in Zen monasteries in twelfth century China. *Chado*, the way of tea, flowed from the principle that the act of making tea could be meditative. It was the tea master Sen Rikyu (1522–91) who organized and blended various styles, philosophies, and procedures of tea customs to form the basis of Chado. At its best, the art of making tea bears eloquent witness to the spirit of *Chado*'s four principles: harmony, respect, purity, and tranquility, which form the practical and highest ideals of the way of tea.

As a Quaker, I take spiritual comfort and learn important life lessons from each stage of tea preparation. Early Friends disavowed so-called "means of grace," such as liturgies and sacramental rites, and some modern Friends may reject the tea ceremony as an outward sacrament. However, for me, *Chado* is a way of focusing the mind through the art of making and drinking a cup of tea. In learning how to become centered as tea host or guest, and in learning how to pay attention to the aesthetics of tea, and to the smallest detail, I connect to *Chado*'s guiding principles—harmony, respect, purity, and tranquility—all values shared by Friends and others.

Harmony

Interaction of host and guest creates the flow of harmony. The tea sweet or meal served with tea complements each season—winter, spring, summer, or fall—and the utensils used for tea create a mood that reflects the season.

Respect

Respect lends structure to the tea ceremony in the form of standard etiquette. Traditionally, in entering the tearoom, jewelry and shoes are removed; one stoops low to enter the small doorway to the teahouse in a sign of humility. We are all one. There is no difference of race, color, or creed, no rich or poor. In holding the tea cup with two hands and bowing gently, we show respect and thankfulness.

Purity

The simple act of cleaning and preparing for the tea service, storing the utensils and cleaning the tearoom, symbolizes purity of heart. In doing so, one is establishing order in the environment and within: attending to the details of the environment, one attends to the mind.

Tranquility

It took years of travel to come to an appreciation of tea and especially Japanese green tea. Throughout my college years, I'd stop each morning before class at a small coffee shop near campus in midtown Manhattan for coffee, light and sweet. For years, I wouldn't even consider drinking coffee unless it was loaded with half and half and three teaspoons of sugar. As I traveled and tasted full-bodied mint tea of Tunisia and Morocco, or the subtle taste of Darjeeling tea of India, or English favorite Earl Grey Tea, I came to appreciate tea, and even adopted new tea customs when I returned home.

Coffee light and sweet became coffee without sugar, which became coffee decaf, which became black tea, which became green tea and homemade chai. In making and drinking tea, I find tranquility in practicing the first three principles of Chado: harmony, respect, and purity. In Japan I discovered that the act of making tea and enjoying it with others or alone can bring a meditative tranquility to the body, mind, and spirit.

As a Quaker, I am called to honor that of God in every person, to live in harmony. I am called to respect and be a good steward of this precious earth. I am called to live in simplicity and restraint to promote ecological and spiritual renewal, knowing the interconnectedness of all things. These general Quaker beliefs are reflected in the principles of tea preparation.

The tea ceremony has much in common with Quaker meeting for worship, where, in the company of many or just a few, gathered together in stillness, confined neither by speech nor silence, I offer myself in communion with God. Meeting for worship provides the structure for understanding Jesus's most basic teachings of faith, love, charity, and honesty. Whether through silent or vocal ministry, in meeting I discern God's call in my life, finding insight and direction. Similarly, in tea preparation, I open to the presence of gracious hospitality and purity of spirit through the simple act of offering a cup of green tea.

Tea preparation is an invitation to spacious awareness. I discover the inner serenity of kindred spirits gathered together to appreciate the gracious simplicity of sharing green tea. In Japan, there is a dramatic form of mime, poetic chanting, and music called *No*. In this theater, the stage may be set with very few props—four pillars, a scroll painting of a pine tree. The primary presence on stage is empty space. Thus, words, movement, or sound, no matter how slight, take on extraordinary significance. It is said that the hidden truth, the essence of life, is expressed in a quality of emptiness, spaciousness. Similarly, through the simplicity and purity of the tearoom, a tone is set of spacious serenity and peace in the careful craft of making green tea. In this state of peace and graciousness of host and guest, attending to every detail with slow, attentive movements, I open the door of the mundane and step into the sacred.

Just as in meeting for worship I wait in quiet expectancy for the call of God's touch, in tea preparation one awaits the presence of guests with open heartedness. Tea preparation cultivates awareness and reflection, focusing attention on the small details: warming utensils, swishing tea, serving a tea sweet to make what could be an ordinary activity sacred. It is a powerful opportunity to renew spirit through harmony with the elements of making and serving tea.

The notion that less can be more at first glance seems counterintuitive. *Chado*, however, reminds me that there is beauty in a simple bowl of green tea.

The essence of the tea ceremony is simplicity; it is acknowledging all that has made the tea gathering possible—the growers of the tea, the sun, wind, and rain, the guests, and the host. The silence of the tea ceremony is punctuated by the wind in the trees or the sound of a bird overhead. This moment was captured by Kakuzo Okakura when he wrote:

> Meanwhile let us have a sip of tea. The afternoon glow is brightening the bamboo, the fountains are bubbling with delight, the soughing of the pines is heard in our kettle, let us dream of evanescence, and linger in the beautiful foolishness of things.

The heart of the tea ceremony is silence and spaciousness, much like that of a Quaker meeting. In the spaciousness of time and the silence that punctuates the tea preparation, words seem unnecessary. Paying exquisite attention to each detail speaks of reverence, and integrity of heart. A harmonious environment opens in this path of tranquility.

I want to take this spirit back home with me. To recall this feeling, I want to put aside the stack of half-finished work projects, the Post-its all over my desk, the pile of clothes to be washed, to keep a promise to myself. Underneath the mounds of to-do lists, I vow to stop to reconsider the ordinary beauty in one cup of tea.

Leaving the park, I continued on to neighboring Shodoshima Island. According to legend, the island was born from a god and goddess. The pilgrimage on Shodoshima is said to be a miniature version of the eighty-eight pilgrimage sites of Shikoku. The thin curve of the new moon hangs low over the craggy peaks of the Setso Inland Sea. This two-day mini-pilgrimage began with a fire ceremony at Emon Fudo Temple, a temple dedicated to Fudo, the God of Light; continued on to Douzan Temple, carved into a rock cave; and ended at Mount Kankakei, where the enormous pure white statue of Kannon dominates the skyline.

The blue-gray mountains on the horizon meet the purplish sky and aquamarine water. Light faded and the slow motion dance of clouds settled.

Buddhist Gatha for Travelers

With each step, I call on the strength and wisdom of Kobo Daishi;
With each step, I open to the kindness of Jizo Bodhisattva;
With each step, I know the all-encompassing compassion of Kannon.
As I purify my hands with this dipper full of water from this stone basin, join my
palms, light this small candle and stick of incense, I offer each act to all those who proceeded me, to those who will follow me and to all those who cannot make this journey;
Hail to all Enlightened Beings throughout space and time.

Practice Lesson of Japan

Next conversation, practice *kanji* (active) listening. Set aside your impulse to fix, solve, correct, or judge the other person. Listen not just with your ears (to hear), but with your eyes (to see), your mind (to think), your heart (to feel), and your attention (to focus). What do you notice about yourself? This builds empathy and compassion, essential tools on the pilgrim's path, and promotes connectedness with others, a fundamental element of *sangha*, community. With this kind of listening, you will never be a stranger.

CHAPTER 5

One River, One Sky, One Earth

Walking in New Zealand

LESSON: Focus on the small, ordinary moment, not the destination.

Rivers are our brothers,
they quench our thirst.

— Chief Seattle

Rivers rule our lives. At times they appear in crevices as a bubble or trickle. They meander in upland pastures, or form braids of water heaving down steep mountain flanks. Rivers flow as spring water, frothing and tumbling in the wild backwoods, forming cloud banks the color of spun gold. Oceans, rivers, streams, creeks, lakes, ponds—New Zealand is this and more. It is a land of water, islands in the far corner of the Pacific Ocean, heavy with the scent of moss and tree ferns, and as special as spiced plum brandy at Christmas time.

Long before this journey to New Zealand, I had read of ancient practices of Australian Aborigines. One sacred legend believes that children, by nature, are in touch with the unseen world and that they remain divided between the spirit realms and physical embodiment for several years before they are completely conjoined with the natural world. This passing from the depths of spirit origin to living consciousness is the path that we all travel and the essence of pilgrimage travel.[12] Pilgrimage is the practice of spiritual alignment of body, mind and soul in the now. It is a way of making meaning of the world around us; of connecting with feelings, emotions and thoughts; of shaking up long-held beliefs and assumptions about people, places and ideas. Pilgrimage is a high stakes enterprise. We are called to connect with what really matters, to rely on judgment and reason and not just heart and soul. Pilgrimage propels us into action, even if that action is taking one step, and then another.

A thin ribbon of morning light is dying into brightness, trimming the horizon—the first sight of the South Pacific as the plane cruised 37,000 feet above the clouds and ocean. The sunlight transformed ice crystals into topaz-studded gems, clinging to the window. The moment the sun rose above the horizon the last tendrils of daylight gave way to blinding, brilliant light—pulsating, radiant white. For hours and hours, miles upon miles, we passed clouds balanced above ocean water, casting jig-saw patterns in slow motion, until we arrived in Auckland.

I came to New Zealand mostly to satisfy my addiction to beauty. My love of beauty is hard to explain. I find beauty in the symmetry of life itself, in the completeness in excavating yet another piece of myself that then leads to a deeper understanding of my place in the world.

When I travel, I love to walk along a sandy beach to discover the hidden treasures of seashells. My Type A mind-set looks for the perfect shell, the one without a crack or a hole. There is a deeper part of me, though, that resists the call to perfection, and that instead very gently picks up the broken shell, still full of integrity, still full of authenticity: I know what it is and I see it for all it is. This is beauty. Travel and especially pilgrimage is

[12] K. Langloh Parker, *Wise Woman of the Dreamtime: Aboriginal Tales of the Ancestral Powers* (Rochester, VT: Inner Traditions International, 1993), p. 91.

sometimes called the great revealer. If we are open to it, we begin to become more aware of ourselves, our fragile thoughts and feelings, our fierce determination, our anger and resentment. I find beauty in the intention and courage to live from one's fountainhead, from that place within that knows what is real, a deep aspiration. I find beauty in ordinary objects—a bowl of pears, or the clean scent of the desert after a sudden rainstorm. Beauty is present in shared moments with friends, in the angle of sunlight on a winter's day, in conflict that turns to understanding, and in the gift of discovery. In pilgrimage one is continually presented with beauty, continually stepping from the known into the unknown, the unexpected moments and places: the wind that pushes hard at my back, the embarrassing encounter with a stranger as I stopped on the side of the road for a pee. The question is: *Where is the beauty in this moment?* I had heard about New Zealand's magnificent scenery, seemingly endless hiking trails, and reliable weather, and I knew this was a place to see at least once in my lifetime, a place to touch beauty.

Auckland is a topsy-turvy array of Australians, Brits, East Indians, the indigenous Maori, who are of Polynesian descent, and others. I came to New Zealand in my late forties, newly married. It was a place that we both wanted to discover together. Our twelve-minute ferryboat ride took us to Devonport, a suburb on Auckland's north shore. It's a picturesque European settlement of early twentieth-century wooden houses, a place of ageless interest. This late spring Sunday afternoon a group of men were playing cricket on an open field. Boys played rugby nearby, scrambling this way and that on the green grass studded with wild daises. People sauntered about for an afternoon stroll along the waterfront promenade, with a southerly breeze to their backs. Couples exchanged love-at-first-sight glances and shared whispered conversations and coffee at trendy sidewalk cafés.

Devonport's gardens, inspiring in a way that something unattainable can be, are a place of rest and enchantment. The scents of hedges of rosemary, lavender, and green santolina extended an open invitation to peek around soft bends. Pink and apricot-colored hollyhocks nestled beside lipstick-red climbing roses. Bushel-sized hydrangea, bronzed fennel, and artichokes complimented another nearby garden. The feathery leaves of the sweet pepper tree cascaded from stone balconies, and prostrate rosemary grew woody and gnarled over rock walls. Curly willow and staghorn ferns held a special place near a back door. It's a lovely walk to shell-strewn Cheltenham Beach with a view of Rangitoto, an 860-foot volcano. On the way back to town, a Brit in an argyle sweater stood at one corner, while on the opposite corner stood a Sikh with a silken navy-colored turban and horned rimmed glasses. This is New Zealand—part Asian, part British, part Polynesian.

National Park

The throbbing vein will
take you further than any thinking.
— Rumi

Our pilgrimage began on the inter-city bus, passed grazing cows that made a checkerboard pattern against the green grass on the road to One Tree Hill. We passed English settlements, like Cambridge, Hamilton, and New Plymouth, and Maori towns of Matamata and Otorohanga, arriving at the ski town of National Park. Our first adventure was tramping (hiking) in Tongariro Crossing, New Zealand's "finest one-day walk." This walk provided a warm-up before John, my husband, and I set off to walk the entire Queen Charlotte Track—forty-five miles from Ship Cove to Anakiwa passing through historic sites, secluded bays and lush coastal bush. We arrived at the base of Tongariro in a bus loaded with other adverterous souls looking to climb the mountain. The driver looked at his watch and said casually, "Be back by 5:00 pm. We leave then. If you're not here, well, I guess you'll have to make your way back as best you can, or just spend the night at the base of the mountain until the morning bus arrives." With a nervous tickle, my husband John and I stared at each other.

Snow nestled in rock crevices as we began our ascent up Tongariro. Nearby rocks were painted with splashes of lichen in orange, red or lime green and volcanic ash powdery as talcum. A frozen hare, a casualty of the bitter cold night, stared up at me, its eyes glistening in the early morning light. I started to get nervous. John looked at me with a steadiness. We passed Scotch broom in full bloom on the roadside and grass the color of burnished copper. Climbing the track of dust, we were at first indifferent to the approaching snow squall. The sky shifted from intermittent clouds, to sun, to rain and wind, then hail, snow and ice, and back to clouds again. The soft green crevasses became snow-and-ice-covered mountainsides. From approaching Mangatepopo Saddle to the summit of Mount Ngauruhoe, volcanic ashen rocks, more a mixture of ash, snow, and ice, blew sideways in the fierce wind. I could barely make out the mountains below. What had been well-placed cairns a few thousand feet below became indistinct blobs of white in blinding, brittle snow.

My boots, caked with snow and ice, were as heavy as dumbbells. For hours we dragged ourselves across ridges and mountain passes, feeling like crap and too frightened to give up, climbing rock over rock, tramping across knife edges, rocky outcroppings and icy ledges, until we reached the base of Mount Ruapehu, doubtful that we had the strength for the summit. I gave up everything except my determination to return to the bus. Alpine flowers closed tight against the fierce hail and snow. Ice and snow clung upside-down to rocks, making geometric patterns in the blizzard. My hands grew numb, in my soaking wet gloves, despite two-ply Polartec and a full Gore-Tex winterized rain suit. And then, just as I thought the worst was over, Tongariro Summit appeared in the distance, a glaciated peak of snow and jagged rock. It was a white-out on the ridge. With pure terror, my breath shortening, the path was a blur of whiteness. I took ten steps wheezing, moving headlong toward the summit, inhaling ice and snow. My heart was thumping: I was flat out terrified. I turned, trying to get a sense of direction, wondering how much steeper and longer until the path disappeared beyond the ridge.

I had forgotten about unrelenting snow. Until now snow was something that softened hard edges, making them pliable and indistinct. It covered regrets and disappointments, it purified dark places, turning slate-gray drab into an abstract mosaic pattern of light. A heavy snow makes a good day to take off from work. Pressing engagements yield to the weight of snow. This snow though was icy-cold, an uncompromising brittle of blue, frozen winteriness, overarching and absolute.

With strange similarity this path is much like the path of practice followed by spiritual seekers. We wander off the path for a moment, an hour, a day, a week, a lifetime. The path of practice consists of noticing and returning. I get discouraged when my mind wanders off the practice. I say, *not again. How many years have I been practicing meditation and my mind still wanders. Can't I get this right?* On the spiritual path, it's not the number of retreats I have attended or the books I have read; it is the humble act of noticing and returning. At this moment, on this pilgrimage, *Where am I now? Take a deep breath into this living moment. Now I am awake, focused.* The next moment—I am lost in thought. The practice is returning, always returning.

Descending Mangatepopo Saddle to Emerald Lakes at five thousand feet, the powdery fine volcanic ash slipped beneath my feet. I slid on my rear end until the earth felt stable enough to hold me. Suddenly, the cloud cover lifted and the vista opened to Emerald Lakes, twin glacial lakes of flawless aquamarine, the color of greenstone. Startled by beauty, I paused to drink in the view.

Pausing is an important transformative practice as a traveler and in life. The Benedictines, like many other spiritual traditions, have a practice of pausing seven times daily to pray—midnight, dawn, mid-morning, noon, mid-afternoon, evening, and night. Pausing is a way of honoring the moment, showing reverence with faithful prayer in our lives. It is this faithfulness—the conscious choice, the commitment to awaken to the goodness in and around us—that heals, that is transformative. As a yoga teacher, I know that pausing is an important part of my practice.

When I first began practicing yoga, I rushed through the transitions from one *asana* (posture) to another, ignoring the moments in between the postures. Coming into, out of, and in between positions felt like nowhere special. The full posture—whether *Virabhadrasana* I (Warrior I) or *Ardha Chandrasana* (Half Moon)—was far more rewarding. When I am aligned in a posture, my bones connect with muscles, and brain, body, mind, and breath unite. In the preparation into or out of a posture, I'm in motion—brain thinking, body moving. In my rush, I found myself more off-balanced, less attentive.

Pausing, as a spiritual practice, has changed the way I do yoga. I give my attention to each movement, moving more slowly, listening as well as feeling. Rushing through transition doesn't stop on the yoga mat. I can't fool myself into believing that this type of forgetfulness is isolated here. Focusing on the transitions strengthens my yoga practice. I feel the full continuum—from the opening to the closing chant. Paying attention to transitions brings life fully alive, and I learn an important traveling lesson: focus on the small, ordinary moments, not the destination. As a traveler, I arrive not once, but again and again.

Descending further from Emerald Lakes to Ketetahi Hut, the uninterrupted landscape of purple-hued mountains cast shadows on deep lakes. We crossed a knife edge at four thousand feet, and crossed narrow mountain paths of snow and ice. My breath grew deep; sweat clung to my Gore-Tex® suit. Arriving at the ranger's hut, there was no time to rest inside for a cup of hot tea, to collect myself for the final descent. We ate our packed lunch, a soggy cheese and fried onion sandwich, standing up.

We walked down steep rock steps, from high alpine fields and rocky summits to scrub bush, down to heather and grassy meadows, down to beech forests of dark green, kauri trees and tree fern forests. Moss clung stubbornly to tree limbs as water rushed everywhere over rocks and roots. It was 4:55 p.m. when we arrived in the waning light at the bus for the ride back to Howard's Lodge, having worked our asses off, legs throbbing, suffering from "survivor's elation."[13] So this was tramping.

National Park to Wellington

In Wellington, New Zealand's capital city, my friend Jonathan met us at the bus station. He, his wife Laura, three daughters, a large terrier poodle, one cat, and three large goldfish, live in an under-renovation, five-bedroom cottage filled with stained glass. The family came to represent the closeness that happens in travel, the strangers one meets by chance that then become life-long friends, the people along the pilgrim's path that lend color and richness to travel. Our visit with them was a brief rest from the trains and boats and seaplanes, and a chance to be with locals, doing local things, blending into the neighborhood. Their cozy home sits perched on the side of one of Wellington's very steep hills in a toney part of town overlooking the harbor. The house is a happenstance of color—red,

---

[13] Annie Dillard, *The Writing Life* (New York: Harper Perennial, 1989), p. 103.

blue-violet, and gray, featuring high ceilings. A stately tree fern grows just outside the front door. The youngest daughter shared her nightly bed with a hot water bottle and a large orange tabby. The middle girl speaks Mandarin and French and is a champion diver and straight-A student. The older girl at fifteen is like most her age, plugged into an iPod, laptop and cell phone. A threadbare sofa in the living room was a cozy nook for the large house pets. The emphasis here is not tidiness, but comfort and homey togetherness. On our first night, we spent hours sitting around the kitchen table with a bottle of *Pinot Grigio* and bowls of homemade New Zealand green mussel chowder. We talked about world affairs, laughing at the indignities of living on the close edge of fifty.

Exploring Wellington

Wellington, the windy city, lived up to its reputation. We were chased everywhere by wind and rain, which also beat against the floor-to-ceiling window in our bedroom. The wind sounded like a turbulent ocean.

In exploring Te Papa, the city's cultural history museum, I began to understand Maori culture and especially the closeness of the people to the land. Maori mythology speaks about the beginning when there was nothingness, *Te Kore*. After nine periods of nothingness came *Te Ata*, the Dawn. From the womb of the darkness came Ranginui, the Sky Father, and Papatuanuku, the Earth Mother. The two were united and bore many children: Tawhiri-matea, the god of wind and storm; Tangaroa, the god of oceans; Tane-mahuta, the god of forests; Haumia-tiketike, the god of wild foods; and Tu-matauenga, the god of war and humans. After eons of living in darkness because their parents were joined together and no light could pass between them, the children decided to separate them so light could enter the world. It was Tane-mahuta who pushed and pushed and succeeded in separating his parents so light could enter the world. The North Island was formed when *Maui*, a demigod, while far at sea, took out his magic fishhook (the jaw of his sorcerer grandmother), tied it to a strong rope, and dropped it over the side of his canoe. He soon caught an immense fish. Beaten with a greenstone club, the fish became the North Island of New Zealand, called *Te Ika a Maui*, the Fish of Maui. The South Island was known as *Te Waka a Maui*, the Canoe of Maui—the canoe he used in fishing. Stewart Island, south of the South Island, was known as *Te Punga a Maui*, the Anchor of Maui, the anchor that held the canoe as Maui hauled the giant fish into the canoe.

Our whirlwind tour of Wellington ended with a celebratory dinner of fish and chips with a splash of ketchup. Adopted by the family in friendship, we each claimed an edge of newspaper and dunked thick wedges of fried potato and fish in ketchup. The grownups capped off the evening with vodka and apple juice and strong mint tea while the city glowed below the kitchen window like a greenstone gem.

Wellington, by Ferry to Picton, the South Island

Leaving Wellington and saying goodbye to Jonathan, Laura, and their three daughters, we boarded the ferry for Picton and the South Island to start our hike on the Queen Charlotte Track. Mountains tumbled steeply down to the aquamarine waters of the Marlborough Sound, an extensive area that includes a maritime park, bays, islands, and other waterways. We sailed for hours through the sheltered bays and deep coves of the living waters of the Queen Charlotte Sound, a part of the larger Marlborough Sound, arriving at Picton, a Maori settlement. Now a maritime city, Picton has become the gateway for exploring the South Island and the Marlborough Sound. This region has quietly become New Zealand's premier wine-growing region with more than thirty vineyards, known for floral Chardonnays, fruity Rieslings and Méthode Champenoise, and Sauvignon Blanc grapevines which make row upon row of sheltered patterns against the cloud-filled sky, while fields of gorse and flax form neat hedges around vineyard properties.

Queen Charlotte Track

We walked the Queen Charlotte Track for five days, 71 kilometers in the heart of the Marlborough and Kenepuru Sounds, on the South Island of New Zealand. The track stretches from Ship Cove, an historic inlet where Captain Cook landed, to Anakiwa, home of New Zealand's Outward Bound program. The coastal track passes through lush tropical forest, studded with tree ferns, around historic bays and along skyline ridges. For five days, we climbed through canopied beech forests, past lookout points, over well-graded bridle paths, following shorelines toward inlets and across high ridges with panoramic views of the Sounds.

The days were clear and clean and the earth was musk-scented. We entered a feathery canopy of tree ferns and tramped over muscle-bound roots of beech trees, enjoying vistas of high mountains and deep coves, cool lakes and green mussel breeding beds. We climbed across grainy, rocky, and muddy paths, sometimes bumbling, through the shade and shadow of the deep forest. On switchbacks, up and down mountains and valleys, we passed cows grazing on hillsides overlooking clear, cool green waters below. At night we were caught by surprise by the stars that glowed in the darkness and blended into the solitude of the sky. I felt light-headed. Perhaps it was the call of the gray warbler in the morning, or the trickle of water down a hillside catching the curled leaves of ostrich fern. There is no "figuring things out," no strategizing or organizing. This time is not about measuring distances, but soaking in each moment. I felt free. But that doesn't matter either. It was just enough to see, sense, and breathe.

Pilgrimage is strongly about place, and the landscape here is everything. I feel lost in the light, the green, green waters that flow everywhere. Here I develop a painterly eye, a way of receiving the world with wide-eyed curiosity from unlikely places.

Picton to Greymouth

Our Atomic Shuttle Minivan putt-putts slowly past the wineries of Blenheim and Picton, the old mining town of Havelock, and the hills and grazing lands of the Rai Valley. We ride on the West Coast road along rocky shores of turbulent turquoise waters, glimpsing intermittently sun and then clouds.

The dusty road meandered past creeks along the roadside, rushing streams that drowned out all sound. Creeks of spring water flowed over rock flakes, beneath train trestles, and beside sheep grazing on the roadside. We crossed Summit Creek and Quinney's Bush, Handrail Creek, Coal Creek, Doctor's Creek, and Flat Ford Creek. There is an unutterable sweetness, a freshness, a timelessness about this land. I feel love-drunk by awareness and beauty, the sun moving behind tree line and the subtle twilight incandescence.

Greymouth to Christchurch

All paths lead nowhere, but one has a heart, the other doesn't.

— Carlos Castaneda

At Arthur's Pass and MacKenzie Country, Scotch broom and wild lupines grew everywhere, trailing into each roadside ditch. Mountain gentians and wild daisies dotted dry riverbeds on the untamed alluvial plains. Clouds tumbled down to mountains, sometimes with a faint clangor, threatening to rain. The

Canterbury Plains, once inhabited by adventurous men digging for gold, are now made notable by mountain ice and snow, frozen lakes, and glacial streams. We took the old stagecoach road, traveling the same roads as hearty souls with a mountaineering spirit who panned for gold or mined coal.

New Zealand is a part of the complex web of life, of energy that is continuously arising and passing away moment-to-moment—the seasons change, night becomes day, cold becomes hot, ice changes to water. The rivers of the North Island affect the glaciers of the South Island. The winds of the Tasman Sea affect the fish in the Pacific Ocean.

Four years before his 1967 Christmas sermon, Martin Luther King, Jr., wrote in jail in Birmingham, Alabama, "It really boils down to this: all life is interrelated. We are caught in an inescapable network of mutuality, tied into a single garment of destiny. Whatever affects one directly affects all indirectly. We are made to live together because of the interrelated structure of reality."[14] This mutuality is interwoven in the fabric of our shared lives on earth.

Thich Nhat Hanh describes this interconnection with a new word, "interbeing," meaning that all life is interconnected, interpenetrating. He teaches that even in a sheet of paper, if one looks deeply, one can see the blue sky, sunshine, and trees. The paper does not have a separate nature, but is a composite of many causes of conditions: water, sunlight, and clouds. Without these elements, the paper would not be possible. Without these nonpaper elements—the sun, the logger who cut down the trees, the rain—there would be no sheet of paper. Therefore, the paper is said to be "empty" of separate self yet "full" of nonpaper elements.[15]

[14] Martin Luther King Jr., *I Have a Dream: Writing and Speeches That Changed the World* (San Francisco: Harper, 1986), pp. 84–100.

[15] Thich Nhat Hanh, *The Sun My Heart* (Berkeley, CA: Parallax Press, 1988), p. 67 and pp. 90–94.

We are connected to all phenomena of the earth. I learned about this interconnectedness at work. For some years, I seldom left the office for lunch. I worked off Route 1 in Edison, an old industrial blue-collar town in central New Jersey. It's gritty and grimy—tractor-trailers, trucks, buses—a mess. One day though I decided to stop at Tastee Sub for a salad sub—the best in New Jersey. (On a visit to the area to promote small businesses, President Obama had stopped by for a turkey and cheese sub.) I move down the assembly line: "Yes, lettuce, tomatoes, peppers, no cheese. Yes, to go." I turn to the cashier and she turns to the guy who just made the sub and says, "Now breathe." At that moment they were my Dharma teachers.

We are all connected to the universal need to infuse the daily grind with moments of awareness. Awareness converts these mechanical acts from mindless repetition to remembering we are alive and life is a miracle. For the traveler, awareness leads to revelatory insights that happen inch by inch in arriving, showing up, being present, learning to be "at home" whether on gritty, grimy Route 1 in Edison or on the beach in Bali. I am continually arriving.

This awareness was beautifully portrayed in the words of John Seed and Joanna Macy in an essay on interbeing.[16] They illustrate our connection to the elements. With water, I am aware of moisture within my body (blood, sweat, tears) and the earth's endless water. With earth, I know that I am made from ashes and dust of the earth and will ultimately return to the earth. With air, as I inhale and exhale, I breathe out carbon dioxide to the trees, and they breathe out oxygen to me. With fire, just as my metabolic fire burns, giving me vital life energy, so too the sun's energy raises the waters on earth and fuels all life. Nature is not something unlike me. It's not something out there, separate and distinct from me. Healing nature means

[16] John Seed, Joanna Macy, Pat Fleming, Arne Ness, *Thinking Like a Mountain* (Philadelphia: New Society Publishers, 1988).

healing the land, not with a "let's-do-something-it's-Earth-Day" sentimentality, but in an effort to heal myself. Healing is an interior gift that connects me with my deepest self. I reach in and find it; I don't reach out and get it. With the grace of healing, I release the long-held resentments, the bitter relations and grudges. I open to immeasurable grace that is all around me and within me. Moving into a quality of presence or "beingness" is about attentiveness at its core. It involves bringing my resourcefulness, values, passion, emotion, and judgment to the moment—a lifetime assignment. My task as a traveler and in life is to walk this path with heart and backbone, to be true to my deepest calling, to move the way courage makes me move and to share this with others.

We traded our public bus for the TranzAlpine scenic train, crossing eastward through the middle of South Island. Our train traversed the Southern Alps climbing high passes and angular mountains, negotiating a labyrinth of tunnels and high train bridges above deep gorges. As the glaciers receded, we followed the Waimakariri River down into the wide expanse of Canterbury Plains, now an area of sheep farming.

Christchurch to Queenstown (via Intercity Bus)

What we need is here.

— Wendell Berry, "The Wild Geese"

Our brief stop in Christchurch, just before sunset, was a chance to visit the botanical gardens. They were nearly empty, except for a few tourists. We were rewarded by the beauty of the rose garden, alive in shades of salmon, red-wine, peach and creamy white.

Back on a bus, the pine forest gave way to sheep grazing in the low grasslands. Fresh fallen snow dusted mountain roads as we descended into the MacKenzie Country, named after early English settlers. The roadside at Irishman's Creek was alive with wild lupine in shades of deep purple, pink, forget-me-not blue, lemony yellow and apricot. A solitary seagull overhead veered right over a turquoise lake. A rainbow faded into the afterglow of the mountains, leaving behind shadows of red, yellow and green. The antique folds of land enveloped us on this our last day in New Zealand.

I reflected on the fragility of wild daisies growing in rocky outcroppings, the pioneer spirit of the men and women who came before me in search of a better life, their labor of love and hard work. Breathing in, I felt the green glow, the purity of this land. Breathing out, I know I will return again.

Alternate Form of the Lord's Prayer from the New Zealand Prayer Book

Eternal Spirit,

Earth-maker, pain-bearer, life-giver,

Source of all that is and shall be,

Father and mother of us all,

Loving God in whom is heaven.

The hallowing of your name echoes through the universe!

The way of your justice be followed by peoples of the world.

Your heavenly will be done by all created beings.

Your commonwealth of peace and freedom sustain our hope and come to earth.

With the bread we need for today, feed us.

In the hurts we absorb from one another, forgive us.

In times of temptation and test, strengthen us.

From trials too great to endure, spare us.

From the grip of all that is evil, free us.

For you reign in the glory of the power that now is love, and forever.

Amen.[17]

Practice Lesson of New Zealand

Eating a meal is often taken for granted as a small, ordinary moment. However, it is a huge opportunity to take pleasure in food and in the sensory experience of eating. Next time you eat lunch, try just eating—not reading, texting, or attending to anything else. Notice the food. Savor flavors. Express gratitude. Put aside thinking about how the food tastes and just experience it. This slows down the eating process, allowing greater awareness, gratitude, and pleasure in the moment. This creates an opportunity to focus on the small, ordinary moments, not the destination.

[17] From the *New Zealand Prayer Book* of the Anglican Church in Aotearoa, New Zealand and Polynesia. Included in *Seasons of Worship at Kirkridge, A Place of Pilgrimage and Prayer*, Kirkridge Retreat and Study Center (June 2007), p. 47.

CHAPTER 6

Pilgrimage to Nearby Places

LESSON: Beauty is closer than you think.

If you love the planet
And you watch the spring come
And you watch the magnolias flower
And the wisteria come out
And you smell a rose

You realize
That you're going to have to
Change the priorities
of your life.

— Helen Caldicott

Pilgrimage journeys need not happen in a foreign country or distant place. A pilgrimage experience is available in our own backyard, a pocket park in town, a nearby garden, or woodland, a familiar road. With all our senses engaged, any journey can lead to awareness and awakening. The writer Margaret Guenther said, "You don't need icons or crucifixes when you are surrounded by the wonder of creation."[18] The sacred is everywhere just waiting to be found.[19]

[18] Margaret Guenther, *My Soul in Silence Waits* (Cambridge, MA: Cowley Publications, 2000), p. 18.

[19] Maria Ruiz Scaperlanda and Michael Scaperlanda, *The Journey: A Guide for the Modern Pilgrim* (Chicago: Loyola Press, 2004) p. 165.

The human spirit needs to pause from the overcommitted, relentless push-pull of contemporary, social media-driven life. Jon Kabat-Zinn, of the Center for Mindfulness in Medicine, Health Care, and Society at the University of Massachusetts Medical School, has noted,

> We have yet to come to grips with the profound and irreversible implications of such technological changes and their effects on the pace of life, the rate, amount and quality of information and images that human beings, even children, have to "process" in a day, the quality of our individual and family lives, the meaning and quality of our work lives and environments, and our greater political and cultural goals and social values. . . . All this technology, although itself potentially enhancing of connectivity and communication is also alienating, intrusive and isolating.[20]

What I crave at times is solitude, not in the sense of personal privacy, but in the deeper sense that Henri Nouwen describes: "a place of conversion, a place where the old self dies and the new self is born," a place of new emergence.[21] This place requires setting space aside to unplug, to take down the scaffolding, close the books, turn off the music, and face nothingness.

My favorite place of solitude is a cloistered nineteenth-century French-inspired convent in a quiet village in central New Jersey—yes, Jersey! Although it is less than a one hour drive from mid-town Manhattan, it remains a place of deep solitude. As I pulled my car into the long gravel driveway and approached the convent one January morning, a lone hawk perched on a chimney greeted me. I took this as a good omen as I climbed

[20] Jon Kabat-Zinn, *Catalyzing Movement Toward a More Contemplative/Sacred-Appreciating/Non-Dualistic Society* (Northampton, MA: The Center for Contemplative Mind in Society, 1994), p. 1.

[21] Henri J. Nouwen, *The Way of the Heart: Desert Spirituality and Contemporary Ministry* (New York, Harper, 1981), p. 27.

the steps, turning the brass doorknob and felt the weight of the oak door. Sister Helen greeted me and showed me to my room, which was furnished with a simple bed, table, chair, dresser, and rocking chair. I sat down on my *zafu*, and felt weightless, like coming back home. I was coming back home to myself. I had put aside all the Saturday chores, the invitations for brunch, the piles of bills and papers stacked on my desk to come here and sit down in the silence. This for me is when the real work of creating a spiritual practice begins: in making the choice, despite all the signals that say otherwise, over and over again, to take the road toward the sacred, to give potency and strength to what is un-nameable.

I was raised Roman Catholic and convents are very special places for me. Even now, I can recall the local parish convent of my childhood at St. Jude: the absolute orderliness; the weightiness of oak and mahogany furniture heavy with silence; the crucifixes and statues of Jesus and an adoring Mary in nearly every room. Everything at St. Jude was real, most especially the oak door of the convent. I can still see myself standing in front of the unpainted door, the knocker aged and heavy, shaped as a cross, the wood carved in Gothic spirals and etched by rain, sun, and snow. I knock on the door. It swings in. There is a moment of doubt: *I don't belong here. I am frightened and curious at the same time.* I realized that walking through the open door at St. Jude's was unlocking a part of my true self, an inner doorway. This was an early taste of hushed silence, the vast presence of a place amplified by prayer.

In Quakerism and Buddhism direct experience is crucial. For Buddhists, we are advised to stay with direct experience without mental elaboration, emotional reactivity, and judgment. This is not to turn one's self into a robot, uncaring and unfeeling, but rather the opposite: to notice and be with feelings and reactions as they arise, to accept them with openness and a quality of friendliness, in a way that builds greater understanding. This is a way of managing one's own emotional state, which frees one's self from the cascade of analysis, worry, second-guessing, rumination, and self-judgment. For Quakers, direct experience of the Spirit is a guide to thought and action. As a Friend, I have seen a gradual realignment of my aspiration with my action, with the Spirit within. For me, it's about aspiration: knowing where, for what purpose, and when to give my energy. These moments of solitude ultimately strengthen the way I live and act in faithfulness to the Light within, much like taking a journey to an unknown place builds trust and faith in the journeying. This realignment has taken me out of the safety and security of my day job as an attorney-lobbyist into the uncharted waters of self-employment. I've traded the big job for big time. This transition informs how I travel, and even how I practice yoga. Traveling as an expression of faithfulness and devotion elevates travel from sightseeing to the sacred. Just the other day, I stumbled along a familiar overgrown footpath. When I came to a clearing on the path, I crossed a footbridge over the river just as the sun was setting in tones of pinkish purple. In an instant, I felt gratitude for the vista before me and behind me. I could have easily missed it, but I didn't. The pilgrim's path is like that. Similarly, yoga becomes an expression of conscious awareness and unity. There is unity, a completeness in coming to terms with the stiffness in my back that doesn't allow me some days to touch my toes. There is peace and contentment in accepting that my left arm may never be able to grasp the right behind my back. Awareness gives rise to acceptance, and acceptance moves us in the direction of wholeness.

From a Buddhist perspective, the first step to healing is to stop, to stop running. The power of stopping, calming, resting, accepting things as they are, even things I don't like, allows me to move to an unaccustomed rhythm. It creates a kind of mental and emotional leisure, ease.

Leisure time—a beach vacation, for example—can be filled with high expectation of a few days away from it all to make up for a lifetime of the mad chase of daily living. I have learned to take frequent mini-pilgrimages to refresh the mind and the spirit, to reconnect with the pilgrim's mind and heart, stepping out of the chronological time and into *kairos* time, suspended in now-ness. One of my favorite mini-pilgrimages is to spend time in my garden at home or to visit a nearby wildflower or woodland garden, especially in early spring.

City Gardens, Woodland Gardens

*Those who don't feel
this life pulling them
like a river, those who
don't drink dawn like
a cup of spring water
or take in a sunset like
supper, those who
don't want to change,
let them sleep.*

— Rumi

A garden is like a heartfelt prayer, and is a pilgrimage place, a place of transformation. To savor a garden in winter or early spring is to fill the senses with anticipation, to whet the appetite with hope for what is to come. The moonlight shimmered glasslike, casting white-purplish shadows through tree branches onto the old brick courtyard of my garden at home, bouncing light off the rhododendron set to bud, cherry laurel, limestone fountain, and teak table and chairs. All was well.

Everything was in place, waiting only for sustained spring, then summer and fall to venture back out into the garden. Here I would enjoy long sunsets in this postage-stamp sized sanctuary, hidden from view behind tall cedar fencing, well back of my 140-year-old home. The textures and sounds lingered in my senses, even after I walked back into the study to take my place at the old pine desk with turned legs.

A garden is never finished. It just keeps evolving and changing, becoming transformed as we transform ourselves. Our gardens grow with each new discovery of some part of ourselves. I learn patience and suddenly I yearn to plant from seeds and not ready-made store bought plants. I learn contentment and know instinctively how to thin plants, to let go of that which is not useful to the plant's vigor. I learn acceptance and tolerance and understand how to till the earth with strength and light hands so as not to damage young plants. I learn gratitude and yearn to share our garden space with beneficial bugs, birds, and butterflies, and even the pesky squirrels, making a home that welcomes them all.

I learned a lot about my level of patience, contentment, and faith too. Shunryu Suzuki, a direct spiritual descendent of Zen Master Dogen, reminds me of the connection between gardening and meditating. He says that the distractions, the "weeds" help strengthen our meditation practice. This is not a philosophical understanding but a direct knowing based on experience. I learned to garden from weeds: the seeds that did not germinate, mint that spread aggressively, native plants mistaken for weeds and pulled out. The practice of *zazen* or Zen meditation creates "weeds" and "flowers" in the mind—the difficult emotion (weeds) and the joyful emotions (flowers). The practice of *zazen* is to keep the mind on the breath and forget everything else—the outcome, the striving, the effect on myself and others. Over time the purity, devotion, and dedication to the practice is transformative, much like putting aside the reams of work to spend the day in a cloistered monastery can create the space for inner transformation.[22]

[22] Shunryu Suzuki, *Zen Mind, Beginner's Mind* (New York: Weatherhill, 1970), p. 37.

Thich Nhat Hanh says that as we touch the earth, and as we walk gently on the earth, it is capable of absorbing all our joy and sorrow. It can support and comfort us. It is not arrogant, vain, humble, or prideful. To walk gently on the earth, to support the earth, to garden is to live fully, because the whole cosmos is present in each blade of grass, each leaf. When we look deeply at a flower, we see not just a flower, but a cloud, the rain, the sun, and the earth, says Nhat Hanh. Without these, the flower would not be possible. Without garbage there would be no compost that enriches the soil that grows flowers. The gardener knows that gardening is embracing interconnectedness, the whole fertility of life, much as the pilgrim embraces the path by her purity of heart, of intention, and of aspiration.

The garden stands as a symbol of culture in a world gone dull and deadened by reality TV and tabloid news. Carl Jung, the Swiss psychoanalyst, described a garden as a symbol of obstacles, hardship, and ignorance that one must overcome in order to attain a higher, divine level of conscious awareness. Cultivation of consciousness and awareness, in Buddhist terms, is the first step in the development of a mind that is concentrated and has clarity, insight, and wisdom. Without awareness, insight is not possible.

Often the most enduring quality of the garden is its ability to heal, to touch me not just at the branches, but deep down at the roots. Too often there is little time to notice a butterfly, to feel the sun's warmth on an early spring day, to really see a flower. This is when the garden sanctuary space takes on deeper meaning. I will never outgrow the need to shelter my heart from business cares and everyday worries. For me, gardens are a part of creating balance, a place to restore child-like wonder. It does not matter much whether the garden is a few well-cared-for plants on an inner-city fire escape, flower boxes brimming with color and texture, or the formal garden of my dreams. I am drawn to finding peace in the gardens, learning the lessons of gardening, and sharing these lessons with others.

Meadows, a Metaphor for Spiritual Journey

In order to understand a flower
you should first observe a flower
blooming in nature, and then
understand this as a metaphor
for the principle of the flower
in all things.

— William Scott Wilson, "The Flowering Spirit,"
Classic Teachings on the Art of Nō

I'm always surprised by the presence of spring. It comes into its own gradually, as if backlit, at a time when winter hands add another log to the fire, the last of the walnut, locust, or oak. Spring rises from the dead end of winter, from scratchy, rough grass and the crevices of time, to make the passerby bend forward to see fiddlehead ferns uncurl or to look under the leaf of the May apple to see its waxy flower.

Long before summer and just after winter, the spring ephemerals appear for the briefest time, perhaps three weeks. The ephemerals, spring's earliest flowers, rise in open fields and country roadsides just before the tender pale green leaves of the birch tree begin to unfold. This is my favorite time to walk in the woods. The earth is fertile and moist, filled with seed and moss. Woodland paths are strewn with the deeply cut leaves of wood poppy, Virginia bluebell, ostrich fern, and spring beauty. Even weedy garlic mustard, purslane, and lamb's quarters invite me to linger for a while, to look again at the honeysuckle-like flower of early wild azaleas. Bluettes scatter thickly across old established moss; the orchid-shaped flowers of the redbud stand as luminous gems against crooked branches. If you are very lucky and know where they grow in the damp woods, you can find giant white trillium or the low-growing spotted leaf of Turk's-cap, twin leaf, jack-in-the-pulpit or yellow lady's slippers. Even skunk cabbage casts bluish shadows in boggy areas or in the chilly mud. Like a prayer answered, in spring I awaken from the strong silence of winter. Physically, my body yearns to explore and grows restless. I feel the urge to move about in the sunlight, to stretch. Emotionally, spring enlivens thinking. Thoughts flow as a stream of mental images. Spiritually, I open to grace within and around me like cool running water in milky moonlight. All of nature seems undeterred by the past months of ice and bitter cold. I feel connected to the earth. The sun's warmth transforms not just me but plants too. Spring's warmth encourages sap in the plant, which later forms the basis of flower and petal, and later still color and fragrance. To walk full of anticipation in a spring meadow—this is no place to hurry.

Meadows, too, offer a metaphor for transformation. They are short-lived, temporary, and yet invite me to linger. Fire or blight clear-cut forests to form a meadow, but not for long. In fifty years or so, it becomes broadleaf forest again through succession. Meadows are alive and dynamic, yet appear unkempt and wild. They may seem empty, but are teeming with life. They are a community of plants with animals like rabbit, fox, deer, birds, butterflies, moths, and insects. As the biodiversity of our countryside quickly disappears to strip malls and McMansions, meadows are becoming rarer.

Meadows remind me that the lessons of change are close at hand. In the face of lives gone numb by predictability, the meadow stands as a wild and unrestrained place. To senses dulled by office-park uniformity, the meadow is a burst of sunlight. To eyes that have narrowed by the regularity of turf grass monoculture, the meadow, with its gay mix of switch grass, Virginia spiderwort, big bluestem, and joe-pye weed, invites me to step into reality.

Just as the meadow cycles back to forest, I too will return to the earth. As with meadows, I am a part of change, transformation, and impermanence, all parts of the pilgrim's path. Paradoxically, the other side of change is stillness on the pilgrim's path. I learned important lessons on the yoga mat that are also useful on the pilgrim's path: allow yourself to fully arrive in a place, to be fully present to beauty that is close at hand. In yoga, a frequent instruction is to hold the pose long enough to feel the benefits of the posture. Often in traveling, I am forward focused. In my zeal to arrive, to get to somewhere, I am looking for the next thing. I learn by going, doing. In pilgrimage travel, I forget and then remember the rewards of being still and being present long enough to bless arriving safely, to bless this place, to gather the meaning and purpose behind the journey.

The seasons of the land have been lost to our awareness. We have forgotten the transition from early spring when ground-nesting birds and mammals establish their territories, to late spring and mid-summer when a rich tapestry of wildflowers provide food for insects and ground-nesting sites for birds, to the ripening of grasses to be cut, dried and baled as hay and carried and stored for winter feed. We have forgotten late summer and autumn, when grass greens up and animals begin to graze again; we have forgotten winter when animals feed on summer hay, and late winter when small amounts of well-aged farm manure are spread on meadows.

As early spring is transformed by sustained warmth, the landscape changes even more. Feral rosebushes, wild red raspberry, sweet pepper bush, magnolia and tasseled grass overtake the ephemerals that wither and fade yellowish into the earth. The sun's warmth invites turtles and frogs to pause in midday.

Buddhism and Nature

"Spring always gives us faith to carry on."
— Thich Nhat Hanh, from *Fragrant Palm Leaves*

Meadows are metaphors for spiritual transformation, and transformation and impermanence are central elements of pilgrimage travel. Hope is the language transformation, and transformation is the nature of life. Nothing is fixed, not even my identity. I am more than my gender, race, religion, occupation, thoughts, and feelings. No matter how bad or good I think a situation is at any moment, it will change. George Bernard Shaw spoke of this when he said, "There are two great disappointments in life: not getting what you want and getting it." I tell myself (on the good days) that I can become whatever I want to be, create the world I want. I keep important questions close at hand: *How do I want to live? What do I value? What does my life stand for?* Again, the lessons of hope are clear. If I can dream, I can hope. I can create. And yet transformation and change can give rise to fear and doubt. I want to resolve what is not resolvable. I strive for more. I want to hold change at bay, want to keep moving on, get caught in negative habits and a self-defeating you-can't-get-there-from-here mentality.

William Bridges in his book *Transitions* reminds me that an important part of any transition is the "empty or fallow time in between" the ending of the old and the beginning of the new. It is the order of nature and an important time for recognizing "endings, lostness and beginnings."[23] It is in this place of lostness, where the familiar gives way to the unknown, where the familiar gives way to the new or where things come apart at the seams, that we may be entering times of real growth. The writer Elizabeth J. Andrew speaks of this loss. She says something like, "The loss of one thing is always a call to develop something else." Pilgrimage is about continual transition: letting go of one vista for another; encountering one stranger and then another; starting out and ending one day and then another. This ending and beginning anew, the in-between moments of

[23] William Bridges, *Transitions, Making Sense of Life's Changes* (Addison-Wesley Publishing Co., 1980), p. 18.

not arriving and not departing is the process of growing the heart. I ask: *How has this moment changed me? Am I present to this moment?*

Sometimes I want to change a lot about myself: to be smarter about money matters, to be more loving, less controlling and judgmental, more forgiving and patient. I have learned though to accept the shape of my life, such as my nagging habits of showing up fifteen minutes or more late for most everything, and putting off paying bills because I hate it, seeing it as a nasty chore. I have accepted, too, the reality that I have stayed too long in a job that feeds my wallet and not my soul, and moved to right the balance. I have accepted my unrealized call toward motherhood, seeing that time has passed me by, while fearing the emptiness of a childless life. My many pilgrimage journeys have molded me into a person with a big heart and lots of courage to meet life head on, full of curiosity, even if with a bit of awkwardness and crankiness. I live with a pilgrim's faith: the faith required to begin, to continue, to finish and to share. I love shedding illusions and facing and naming what is. I even love the lost-in-the wilderness moments, the can't-get-there-from-here moments, the pent-up moments of unplanned joy. As a pilgrim, I have practiced (not perfected) the rules of the road: the discipline of listening deeply and seeing, not just as a way of receiving information, but of being.

Again with elegant simplicity, Shunryu Suzuki reminds me that the most basic teaching of Buddhism is that "everything changes." Buddhist texts caution me on placing happiness on that which is subject to change, to external conditions (the right mate, the right job, the right house), on avoiding discomfort, pain, and suffering. Buddhist practice is instructive for pilgrims. It urges me to embrace pleasure and pain: both the days when I make all the right travel connections and the days when my luggage is lost in a distant airport. These are tools of an awakened traveler.

Though it may seem counterintuitive, among the first steps of spiritual path is to move into pain, doubt, discomfort, and resistance. When I am fully awakened to the depth of my experiences—pleasure and pain—nothing more is needed. Oddly, the moment is full. In this fullness I am better able to accept difficulties with less drama. This does not mean that I do not have preferences and do not wrestle with things the way they are. It means that I allow my *reaction* to become a part of my awakening, and to accept it all. I soothe myself and tell myself that I have all that I need to face the doubts, pain, discomfort, and resistance. Holding the frustrations, disappointments, and hurts tenderly allows me to open to them and struggle less, and even in the face of these questions: *Can I sit with life's unpredictability, and let that be? Is the struggle to live in faithfulness really worth it, especially when I can't even name what is resting on my heart? What do I trust when my just-the-facts mentality comes face to face with part of me that seeks inner oneness?* The pilgrim's path teaches me to be happy, even when the circumstances of my life aren't painful, and to know that happiness is much deeper than external events.

The lesson for the traveler is clear whether the journey is by foot, or by plane, car, bicycle, or ship, whether the journey is around the world or around the corner. The journey itself, the events and emotions, the land and the people one meets along the way, is its own reward, and each encounter has the potential for greater meaning if I see and feel with a pilgrim's eyes and heart. The road itself is healing—to find contentment in the lonely dinners in a strange city; to climb to the top of a sacred site expecting a solitary experience only to find it claimed by hundreds of others; to find strength when my arms and legs are weary from dragging backpacks and suitcases from one place to the next.

The Buddha said that if you want to see what's really going on in your life, what's really important, then forget the grand, abstract spiritual questions and focus on what you're doing right here and right now. Pay close attention. As a traveler this means to see, to feel, to taste and touch, to make peace with myself and the nature of things, to discover hope in the grit of the road.

Pilgrims do not need special language, a special journey, or a special time of year, although spring, with its hope of birth and renewal, is always good. The spiritual path, the pilgrim's path, the path of Light within, is about becoming more of what I am meant to be. As I become more myself, I see the union of all things. My calling is to be drawn closer and closer toward Love. This is transformation and integration. Who I am, what I believe, and my actions align. The Buddha's teachings, over 2,500 years ago, of compassion, understanding, love, and equanimity are available to me here and now. I need only turn toward them. This turning with open heart is called grace among Christians. Early Friends advise that our lives are not meant to conform to a set of secular rules, but to "Obedience to the Light." Whether I find meaning in the journey itself, arriving at a long-sought-after destination, recalling a journey, or journeying not far from home, the pilgrim's way is the outward seeing and the inward being. It is mindful attention and mindful intention. It is the effort to be companions to all of nature, a moving toward oneness with this whole spectacular universe.

I started these pilgrimage journeys seeking meaning and purpose to my life, searching in far-off places. I took a leap of faith into the unknown. The sheer vulnerability of travel left me open to immense joy and immense frustration. The pilgrim's path is one of action and presence. It is the path of letting go, showing up, trusting, slowing down, listening, facing fears, learning the pleasure of play, and so much more. These life lessons learned across the world were re-discovered close to home.

Pilgrimage is a life-affirming process, a creative undertaking that gifts us with the fullness of life itself.

Buddhist Gatha

Guide my tired feet, oh God
Guide my expectant hands, Lord Buddha
Guide my heavy heart, Lord Krishna
Guide my busy mind, Yahweh
Guide me on this pilgrim's path

Practice Lesson of Pilgrimage to Nearby Places

Take a walk in a nearby park. Plant a small garden or pot of flowers or herbs, and tend to it. Notice how you feel while walking and while gardening. Pause. Take in what is happening. Notice the beauty that is close at hand. This strengthens awareness, the building blocks of mindfulness. This links us to a quality of interconnectedness Buddhists call "interbeing": the realization that we do not live in isolation, we are part of an intricate fabric of life. Paying attention for what is beautiful in daily life expands the heart.

El Camino Training Schedule

Sunday	Walk 3–4 miles mostly uphill with 20-pound pack
Monday	Walk or bicycle 30 minutes to 1 hour Meditate 2 hours
Tuesday	Walk 30 minutes Lift weights 30 minutes Use steam room 10 minutes
Wednesday	Kundalini yoga 1.5 hours Meditate 2 hours
Thursday	Walk or bicycle 30 minutes Lift weights 30 minutes Use steam room 10 minutes
Friday	REST
Saturday	Walk 5-6 miles mostly uphill with 20-pound pack 2 to 3 hours Use steam room 10 minutes

Sample Packing List

(For Walking in October)

1   Pair well broken-in hiking boots

2   Pairs wicking--type cushioned socks

2   Pairs wicking--type sock liners

1   Mole foam

1   Moleskin

1   Lamb's wool

1   Hiking pole

1   Pair lightweight sandals

2   Running bras—wicking type

3   Wicking-type underpants

1   Wicking-type mid-weight underwear (black)

1   Wool hat

1   Pair wool gloves

1   Gore-Tex® rain jacket and pants

1   Bandana

1   Rucksack and rain cover

2   Long sleeve wicking-type shirts (black)

1   Short sleeve wicking-type shirt (black/gray)

1   Long quick-dry pants (black)

3   Water bottles and camel pack

1 Watch

1 Traveling alarm clock

1 Small toothpaste

1 Tooth brush

1 Small plastic bottle of lotion

1 Hair brush and hair clip

1 Lipstick

1 Lip balm

1 Face powder

1 Chinese remedy for upset stomach

1 Chinese remedy to prevent colds

1 Vitamin pack containing: Vitamins A, B, C, E, Folic Acid,
Zinc, Melatonin, Magnesium, Fish Oils, Glucosamine
Sulfate, MSM, Acidophilus

1 Pen knife (for cutting cheese and mole foam)

1 Extra bootlace

1 Space blanket

1 Sunglasses

1 Pair contact lenses and case

1 Contact lens wetting and soaking solution

1 Camera

1 Notebook and 3 pens

1 Passport, wallet, money

1 Pilgrim's credentials

Travelers' Resource Guide
My Top Picks

The list below includes my choices of the best traveling resources. I have found these resources to be consistently reliable and invaluable when planning, scheduling, and traveling.

Best Airline Ticket Booking

- ○ www.Kayak.com

Best Travel Guide Books

- ○ The Lonely Planet Travel Guides, **www.lonelyplanet.com**
- ○ The Rough Guides, **www.roughguides.com**

Best Large Tour Operators for Travel Worldwide

- ○ HF Holidays—This award-winning company, the U.K.'s largest hiking and leisure activity tour company, offers worldwide trips geared toward active persons and groups. Specializes in the United Kingdom and Europe. **www.hfholidays.co.uk**
- ○ Overseas Adventure Travel—Offers small group travel with a focus on adventure and value. 1-800-493-6824
- ○ Explore!---Specializes in small group, worldwide destinations. 1-800-715-1746. **www.exploreworldwide.com**

Best Small Tour Operators for Travel Worldwide

- ○ Celtic Journeys—Operated by the Community of St. John Baptist, Mendham, NJ. Specializes in small-group spiritually inspired tours of the United Kingdom. **www.celticjourneys.org**

- ○ Kirkridge Retreat and Study Center—Offers spiritual pilgrimages worldwide. Specializes in pilgrimages to Iona, Scotland and New Mexico. **www.kirkridge.org**

- ○ Appalachian Mountain Club—Offers major excursions worldwide geared toward hiking, and other outdoor activity. **www.outdoors.org/majorexcursions**

- ○ Eleven Directions—Offers spiritual tours of India with a focus on mindfulness and Buddhism. **www.buddhapath.com**

- ○ Myths and Mountains—Specializes in Southeast Asia and South America with a focus on people and culture. **www.travel@mythsandmountains.com**

- ○ The Wayfarers—Specializes in all-inclusive walking vacations especially in the United Kingdom and Europe. **www.thewayfarers.com**

Best Large Educational Tour Operators

- ○ Smithsonian Journeys—Offers worldwide educational tours. **www.smithsonianjourneys.org**

- ○ Geographic Expeditions—Offers high-end, customized once-in-a-lifetime trips to far corners of the world. **www.geoex.com**

Best Large Ecotour Operator

- ○ Earthwatch Expeditions—Work alongside scientists all over the world. **Expeditions@earthwatch.org www.Earthwatch.org**

Best Small Ecotour Operator

- African Summer Workcamps, African Great Lakes Initiative of Friends Peace Teams—Offers intergenerational workcamps in Africa. **www.aglifpt.org**
- Costa Rica Study Tours—Focus on Quaker community in Costa Rica. **www.crstudytours.com**

Best Caribbean Vacation

- Villa Arcadia—Located adjacent to a private cove, facing the ocean, this serene cottage sits on one acre of farmland in Jamaica's hidden gem---Treasure Beach. **www.homeaway.com**

Best Travel Rucksack

- Mountainsmith **www.mountainsmith.com**

Best Travel Clothing

- TravelSmith **www.TravelSmith.com**

Best Vacation in the Southwest United States

- Ghost Ranch, a 21,000-acre education and retreat center operated by the Presbyterian Church, offers a place to rest and renew the spirit. Painter Georgia O'Keeffe lived nearby. **www.ghostranch.org**

Best Movie on Pilgrimage

- *The Way* is a powerful and inspirational story about family, friends and the challenges we face while navigating this ever-changing and complicated world. Martin Sheen plays Tom, an irascible American doctor who comes to France to deal with the tragic loss of his

son (played by Emilio Estevez). Rather than return home, Tom decides to embark on the historical pilgrimage "The Way of St. James" to honor his son's desire to finish the journey. What Tom doesn't plan on is the profound impact this trip will have on him. Through unexpected and oftentimes amusing experiences along "The Way," Tom discovers the difference between "the life we live and the life we choose."
www.theway-themovie.com

Best Travel Movie

- ○ *The Best Exotic Marigold Hotel*—British retirees travel to India to take up residence in what they believe is a newly restored hotel. Less luxurious than its advertisements, the Marigold Hotel nevertheless slowly begins to charm in unexpected ways.
  www.foxsearchlight.com/thebestexoticmarigoldhotel/

Author's Photograph Resource

- ○ See some photos from the author's travels at
  http://leadsmartcoaching.com/photo-gallery-2.

ABOUT THE AUTHOR

Valerie Brown is a leadership coach, leadership educator, retreat leader, and principal of Lead Smart Coaching, LLC. She is a member of the Religious Society of Friends (Quakers), and has studied and practiced Buddhism since 1995 with Thich Nhat Hanh. She is the author of several publications on mindfulness, including *Living from the Center, The Mindful Quaker* and *Heartfulness: Renewing Heart, Mind and Spirit on Retreat and Beyond.* Her work and writing point toward powerful transformation through mindful awareness, and her passion is for creating greater trust, authenticity, and integrity among people worldwide. She lives in bucolic Bucks County, Pennsylvania, with her husband John. Contact her at **www.leadsmartcoaching.com.**

CPSIA information can be obtained at www.ICGtesting.com
Printed in the USA
BVOW021620130912

300310BV00002B/2/P